DISCARDED

Black-Jewish Relations in New York City

PRAEGER SPECIAL STUDIES IN
U.S. ECONOMIC AND SOCIAL DEVELOPMENT

Black-Jewish Relations in New York City

Louis Harris
Bert E. Swanson

PRAEGER PUBLISHERS
New York · Washington · London

The purpose of Praeger Special Studies is to make specialized research in U.S. and international economics and politics available to the academic, business, and government communities. For further information, write to the Special Projects Division, Praeger Publishers, Inc., 111 Fourth Avenue, New York, N.Y. 10003.

PRAEGER PUBLISHERS
111 Fourth Avenue, New York, N.Y. 10003, U.S.A.
5, Cromwell Place, London S.W.7, England

Published in the United States of America in 1970
by Praeger Publishers, Inc.

All rights reserved

© 1970 by Louis Harris and Bert E. Swanson

Library of Congress Catalog Card Number: 71-124862

Printed in the United States of America

CONTENTS

Page

THE STUDY: DESIGN AND METHODS — vii

    Questionnaire Design — viii
    Sample Design and Weighting — viii
        Sampling Errors for Estimated Percentages — xi
    Interviewing — xi
    Definition of Groups Analyzed — xii
        Jews — xii
        Blacks — xiii
        Non-Jewish Whites — xiv
        Puerto Ricans — xv
        Special "Backlash" Sample of Non-Jewish Whites — xv

INTRODUCTION: NEW YORK, CITY OF MINORITIES — xvii

Chapter

1   TENSION AND CONFLICT — 3

    The Reality of Tension and Conflict — 3
        Feelings Behind Views of Black-Jewish Relations — 4
    How Blacks and Jews Look at the Establishment — 9
    The Roots of Tension and Conflict Among Jews — 10
    The Roots of Tension and Conflict Among Blacks — 23

2   A COMMON BOND: PERCEPTIONS OF DISCRIMINATION — 27

    Discrimination Against Jews — 27
    Discrimination Against Blacks — 36

3   HOW BLACKS ARE PERCEIVED — 42

    "Tearing Down White Society" — 45
    Integration or Separation? — 53
    Are Black Demands Justified? — 61

		Page
	Pace of Blacks in New York City	64
	Discrimination Against Blacks	71
	Police Treatment of Blacks	82
	Concern in Certain Situations	91
	Stereotypes About Blacks	96
	Black Anti-Semitism	104
4	HOW JEWS ARE PERCEIVED	108
	Positive and Negative Stereotypes	108
	What Blacks and Non-Jewish Whites Say About Jews	118
	Jews Estimate Anti-Semitism	122
5	THE TRIGGER OF POLARIZATION: THE NEW YORK CITY SCHOOL DISPUTE	131
	"Harlem on My Mind"	153
	Vandalism Against Synagogues	156
6	POTENTIAL AREAS OF CONFRONTATION	159
	Building Trades Employment for Blacks: Potential Confrontation with Non-Jews	159
	The Welfare Crisis	162
	News Coverage	179
7	INTERGROUP CONTACT: REAL OR PERCEIVED?	185
8	THE ACTION OPTIONS OPEN TO BLACKS AND JEWS	205
	Black Approaches to Action	208
	Approaches Within the Jewish Community	220
	A Final Observation	230
ABOUT THE AUTHORS		235

THE STUDY: DESIGN AND METHODS

The Ford Foundation through the Institute for Community Studies at Sarah Lawrence College commissioned Louis Harris and Associates to conduct a study of black-Jewish relations in New York City. Several events in recent years, and especially the 1968 teacher strikes and their aftermath, have made this a subject not only of real interest in itself, but also of real importance to the direction in which New York City moves--in its politics, in its mood, in its intergroup relations.

The research, which took place in late April and May 1969, had six basic aims:
   1. To determine the points of contact between blacks and Jews in New York City.
   2. To delineate among these the current and likely future points of misunderstanding or conflict between the groups.
   3. To determine the current and likely future points of empathy and cooperation between the groups.
   4. To investigate, in depth, the attitudes underlying the areas of conflict and cooperation.
   5. To investigate the attitudes and perceptions of the non-black, non-Jewish population of the city on the same issues.
   6. To similarly investigate a special sample of non-Jewish whites in New York City likely to hold "backlash" attitudes.

Of course, there are many ways of looking at New York. It can be seen in terms of its five boroughs; of the different age groups, classes, and levels of educational achievement in its population; of its ethnic make-up. Obviously no one perspective alone can explain the intricacies of this complex city. This study attempted to look at New York's attitudes in a number of different ways.

At the same time, however, this study does place a special emphasis on looking at New York City in ethnic terms. There are many reasons for this. It extends from the subject we were asked to study, black-Jewish relations. It grows out of the way New Yorkers--on the street, on television, in newspapers, and in learned journals--have talked about recent intergroup conflict in their city. It reflects a crucial aspect of the reality of this city's life; as Nathan Glazer and Daniel Patrick Moynihan observed in <u>Beyond The Melting Pot,</u> "many elements--history, family and feeling, interest, formal organizational life--operate to keep much of New York's life channeled within the bounds of the ethnic group."* And it is a perspective that, we believe, the results of our study substantiate--both as a useful way of looking at the city and as a helpful way of moving toward reconciliation.

The focus of this study was to neither please nor annoy. In the past, ethnic labels have often aroused deep emotions. All we can say in response is that we have tried to present the survey's findings and their implications as honestly and as objectively as possible.

QUESTIONNAIRE DESIGN

The questionnaires were designed by Louis Harris and his staff in cooperation with Bert Swanson of the Institute of Community Studies at Sarah Lawrence College and his staff. Three questionnaires were constructed: one for the black population, one for the Jewish population, and one for non-Jewish whites in the city.

Each questionnaire had certain items uniquely applicable to its own target group, other items which were identical in the three questionnaires to allow for direct comparison of all groups, and a third group of items which were parallel but not identical, e.g., an item asking Jews how they thought blacks feel on a particular issue, which could be compared to a parallel item asking blacks how they actually feel.

The questionnaires were revised on the basis of a pretest with a selected sample of 50 people throughout the city before the final data collection began.

SAMPLE DESIGN AND WEIGHTING

The population universe in this survey was made up of adult residents of New York City. Because the black and Jewish communities were the central focus in this study, an oversample of each of these groups was included in the survey. In addition to these groups, oversample of "backlash" areas (as represented by the vote on the Police Civilian Review Board) was also included.

---
*Cambridge, Mass.: MIT Press, 1966, p. 19.

Thus four separate samples were constructed. The first sample was a probability sample of households in New York as tabulated in the 1960 Census material. The oversample of blacks (86 sample points, 860 interviews) used Census tracts with at least 50 percent black population in 1960. The Jewish oversample (45 sample points, 450 interviews) was based on a study of the percentage of Jewish population in each of the assembly districts of the city. This information was used to construct a frame, including certain detailed information within the assembly district, to construct a random sample of areas showing a high proportion of Jews within the area. The average proportion of Jews within the area sample was approximately 64 percent. The sample of the "backlash" area (30 sample points, 300 interviews) was drawn from election districts whose vote against the civilian review board exceeded a 4-to-1 margin--the review board was defeated city-wide by a 2-to-1 margin.

The basic sample of households in the city was stratified by borough. Within each borough a random sample of census tracts was selected, the probability of a tract being selected being proportional to the number of households within that tract. Once a tract was selected a block was chosen at random; again, the probability of a block being selected was proportional to the number of households in the block. If the number of households in the block was under 50, the contiguous block whose Census tract block number was the next highest was used. Only one interview was conducted in each household, and the respondent within the household was selected by a random device.

In this basic sample, no provision was made for interviewing any special group in the population. The three oversamples were drawn from the groups most relevant to this study (see Table 1).

The black oversample was chosen using basically the same material and methods. Since the census figures provide a racial breakdown of the population, it was possible to isolate those areas of heavy black concentration. The criterion used for isolating a particular census tract was that it be at least 50 percent black. Once the original universe was reduced, the same statistical methods as in the basic sample were used to randomly choose 86 census tracts as sample points. Again, these sample points were divided among the boroughs proportionally to black population.

The Jewish oversample was designed on the basis of the percentages of Jews living in each assembly district in the city. Five figures were available for each assembly district,

TABLE 1

SAMPLE POINTS BY BOROUGH[a]

Borough	Basic Sample	Oversamples		
		Blacks	Jews	"Backlash"
Manhattan	26	34	10	1
Bronx	18	7	8	4
Brooklyn	32	32	16	10
Queens	22	13	11	12
Richmond	2	--	--	3
Total	100	86	45	30

[a] Ten interviews were scheduled for each sample point.

indicating five (or more) different sections of the assembly district. This was particularly helpful because many of the assembly districts in the city (especially in Brooklyn and Queens) cover large and ethnically varied areas. Sample points were randomly chosen from those areas which showed significantly high proportions of Jews (averaging 64 percent Jewish). The sample points were divided among the boroughs according to percentages of Jewish population obtained from the same study.

The oversample of non-Jewish whites likely to hold "backlash" sentiments regarding issues of civil rights was defined in terms of the returns of the 1966 city-wide referendum on establishing a civilian review board for the Police Department. The over-all result of the referendum was defeat of the review board by a margin of roughly 2 to 1; the oversample population was defined as residents of those election districts which opposed the review board by at least a 4-to-1 margin. The 30 sample points were divided proportionally to the number of election districts showing a 4-to-1 defeat of the review board in each borough. Election districts in each borough were then chosen randomly as sample points.

Because of the design of the sample, it was necessary to weight the results to obtain an appropriate representation of the residents of New York City. This weighting was accomplished to bring the ethnic composition of the sample into line with the assumption that in the city, the population consists of 25 percent Jews, 20 percent blacks, and 55 percent other groups. For the purposes of weighting, the "backlash" sample was excluded and the results from this sample were not combined with the other samples.

Sampling Errors For Estimated Percentages

It is not possible to obtain exact sampling errors for all the characteristics considered in the survey. The following list provides a guide to the estimated percentage errors for certain size bases; the values shown are estimates of the largest deviation to be expected (at a 95 percent level of confidence) from the reported percentages for the indicated base:

Base	Deviation
100	12%
250	8%
500	6%
1,000	4%

INTERVIEWING

Because of the emotional content of the study, particular attention was given to the training and briefing of the interviewers. Briefing sessions with the interviewers were held by the supervisory staff of Louis Harris and Associates. The questionnaires were analyzed and rehearsed, item by item, with the interviewers in order to minimize any possible biasing effects in their interview technique and to prepare them for respondent reactions which might invalidate the interview or bias the sample.

Interviewing took place between April 25 and May 20, 1969. In over 90 percent of the cases, white interviewers interviewed whites and black interviewers interviewed blacks. The average interview lasted one and one quarter hours.

In order to insure a representative sample, each interviewer was assigned an area, precisely defined and limited, from which all his interviews had to come. These areas ("sample points") were, on the average, three to four square blocks. In addition to geographical restrictions, interviewers were bound by a number of other guidelines designed to minimize bias in the selection of respondents. These included procedures which randomized the selection of the interviewee within a household, which prevented an oversampling of unemployed or retired males at home during the day, which avoided "volunteer respondents," and which insured an equal chance for selection for each household in a sample point.

In addition, each interviewer's work was checked to make sure interviews had been conducted as reported.

DEFINITION OF GROUPS ANALYZED

A total of 2,486 questionnaires was analyzed--634 Jews, 1,041 blacks, 511 non-Jewish whites (including 131 Puerto Ricans), and a special sample of 300 non-Jewish whites from areas voting overwhelmingly against the civilian review board in 1966.

This special sample of 300 non-Jewish whites was analyzed separately at all times. The other three groups were analyzed separately and an additional analysis was made of their total (2,186) weighted responses which represented the population of New York City: Jewish, 25 percent; black, 20 percent; non-Jewish whites, 55 percent.

By borough, 28 percent of those interviewed in the survey came from Manhattan, 16 percent from the Bronx, 23 percent from Queens, 31 percent from Brooklyn, and 2 percent from Richmond.*

Following are definitions of the subgroups analyzed within each of the samples.

Jews

The total sample of Jews was 634. The breakdown among Jews interviewed in the survey is:

---
*Because of the small size of the Richmond sample, it is only analyzed in the total weighted responses.

By borough: 20% Manhattan
19% Bronx
26% Queens
35% Brooklyn
By religion: 16% Orthodox
35% Conservative
21% Reform
28% "non-affiliated" or "not sure"
By age: 34% 21-34 years old
25% 35-49 years old
42% 50 years old or above
By income: 47% under $10,000 total family income in 1968
28% $10,000-$14,999 total family income in 1968
25% over $15,000 total family income in 1968
By education: 13% 8th grade or less
40% high school (more than 8th grade but no college)
47% college (at least some college)
By sex: 51% male
49% female

Blacks

The total sample of blacks was 1,041. The breakdown among blacks interviewed in the survey is:
By borough: 32% Manhattan
13% Bronx
15% Queens
40% Brooklyn
By age: 42% 21-34 years old
36% 35-49 years old
22% 50 years old or above
By income: 19% under $3,000 total family income in 1968
51% $3,000-$6,999 total family income in 1968
30% $7,000 or above total family income in 1968
(21% with a family member now receiving welfare)

By education: 20% 8th grade or less
65% high school (more than 8th grade but no college)
15% college (at least some college)
By sex: 49% male
51% female

Non-Jewish Whites

Within the regular New York City sample, a sample of 511 non-Jewish whites was taken. The breakdown among non-Jewish whites in the regular sample is:

By borough: 32% Manhattan
15% Bronx
24% Queens
27% Brooklyn
2% Richmond
By religion: 75% Catholic
25% non-Catholic
By ethnic group:* 21% Italian
9% Irish
26% Puerto Rican
By age: 40% 21-34 years old
34% 35-49 years old
26% 50 years old and above
By income, Catholic:
13% under $5,000 total family income in 1968
53% $5,000-$9,999 total family income in 1968
34% $10,000 and above total family income in 1968
By income, non-Catholic:
21% under $5,000 total family income in 1968
47% $5,000-$9,999 total family income in 1968
32% $10,000 and above total family income in 1968
By education: 75% no college education
25% at least some college education
By union membership: 39% with a family member in labor union
By sex: 53% male
47% female

---
*Reported birthplace of grandparents.

Puerto Ricans

Of the 511 non-Jewish white sample, 131 were Puerto Rican. The breakdown among Puerto Ricans in the regular non-Jewish white sample is:
By borough: 53% Manhattan
26% Bronx
1% Queens
20% Brooklyn
By age: 47% 21-34 years old
42% 35-49 years old
11% 50 years old and above
By religion: 95% Catholic
5% non-Catholic
By education: 95% no college education
5% at least some college education
By union membership: 35% with a family member in labor union
By sex: 49% male
51% female

Special "Backlash" Sample of Non-Jewish Whites

The total special sample of non-Jewish whites from election districts voting more than 4-to-1 against the Civilian Review Board was 300. The breakdown among the special sample of non-Jewish whites is:
By religion: 78% Catholic
22% non-Catholic
By ethnic group:* 30% Italian
17% Irish
By age: 38% 21-34 years old
28% 35-49 years old
34% 50 years old or above
By education: 80% no college education
20% at least some college education
By union membership: 44% with a family member in labor union

---

*Reported birthplace of grandparents.

By occupation:*   23% professional, executive
                    16% white collar
                    30% skilled labor
                    21% unskilled labor
By sex: 51% male
          49% female

---
*Occupational classification of head of household.

INTRODUCTION: NEW YORK, CITY OF MINORITIES

There are really two New York Cities. One is the major center for communications, finance, corporate decision-making, and the arts in the United States. The residents of this New York City form the highest concentration of the power elite in the United States and probably in the world. The population of this city is no more than 500,000 at best. Most of its activities take place on the island of Manhattan, though many of this elite do not even live in the city itself.

The other New York City consists of over 7,000,000 people, spread over five boroughs from Staten Island in the south to the Bronx line in the north, to Brooklyn, and eastward to the reaches of Queens.

This study is basically about the New York City which has a minority of the power but a majority of the population. In many ways this New York City is a series of contrasts and anomalies. It would be difficult to find a combination of ethnic groups more atypical of the United States. In the country as a whole, white Protestants dominate in numbers, totaling close to two out of every three Americans. In New York, WASPs are no more than 6 percent of the adult population, a small minority highly visible in the power elite but of marginal significance in terms of numbers.

White Catholics are the largest group in the city. People of Italian descent are the most numerous of the Catholics, with 14 percent of the city's population. Those whose ancestors came over from Ireland make up 8 percent. Often ignored is the sizable German-descended population, estimated at 10 percent. The remaining white Catholics trace their origins back to southern, central, and eastern Europe.

In the aggregate, white Catholics make up 38 percent of New York's population. This percentage is less than it was at the start of the 1960's, when Catholics constituted an estimated 45 percent. As they have become more affluent, many have migrated out north across the Bronx line to the sprawling suburbs of Westchester and eastward to help fill up Nassau and Suffolk Counties out on Long Island; and some have crossed the Hudson River to Bergen County in New Jersey.

The second largest group are the Jews, who make up an estimated 25 percent of the city's adult population. They, too, have declined in numbers in recent years, from 30 percent at the start of the 1960's. In concentration, the Jewish group still is most populous in Brooklyn but has lost its position as a majority of that borough. The most affluent Jews live in Manhattan, the least affluent in the Bronx, where their traditional neighborhoods have been inundated by in-migrations of Puerto Ricans and blacks. The Jewish population of Queens has been increasing. Largely a bedroom community, Queens represents for many Jews a step up from the old neighborhood in Brooklyn and the Bronx, perhaps on their way either to the suburbs or to Manhattan.

Easily the fastest growing segments of New York City are the blacks and Puerto Ricans. Among the adult population, blacks number 20 percent, while the Puerto Rican population is an estimated 11 percent. This means that close to one third of the city can be counted as either black or Puerto Rican. And both groups have grown rapidly. Whereas at the beginning of the 1960's blacks made up an estimated 14 percent of the population, by the end of the decade this percentage had grown by approximately half. Puerto Ricans made up no more than 5 percent in 1960; this percentage doubled by the end of the decade.

The blacks and Puerto Ricans are concentrated in the older sections of Manhattan, Brooklyn, the Bronx, and, to a lesser extent, Queens. Staten Island is close to 100 percent white. The blacks and the Puerto Ricans, as the last to arrive, have been the last to find employment when they can. They make up a majority of the city's burgeoning welfare rolls. They live in the poorest housing, have the most unemployment, and are concentrated in the highest crime areas.

Traditionally, the key to New York City has been its ethnic makeup. New Yorkers have lived in their own enclaves, largely demarcated by ethnic lines. Whole stretches of any borough today can be observed as not only black or Puerto Rican, but also Jewish, Italian, and to a disappearing degree, Irish. There are also smaller concentrations of Scandinavians, Greeks, Lebanese, Poles, Chinese, and other ethnic strains. These latter groups are hardly visible, for it takes sizable numbers to make a noticeable dent in New York's population statistics.

During most of the 19th century and the first half of the 20th, as a new group arrived in the city, it would stake out a neighborhood, welcome its kinfolk, and settle in for the long pull. The city's history is replete with accommodations being made among the various ethnic strains to allow each to find its own center of gravity.

At times, the crowded city has given vent to sharp antagonisms along ethnic lines. Jewish-Irish divisions often were not far below the surface. Within the Catholic group, tension between Irish and Italians appeared with some frequency. But for the most part New York's ethnic groups have followed an unwritten rule: survival in the city requires minorities to stick together and find ways of accommodating each other. Otherwise, the city would fall apart. As a result, what might have become a boiling cauldron, because of wide differences between minorities with distinct cultural pasts and tastes, came to be called proudly (if not entirely accurately) the great melting pot.

This essential element of accommodation should not be underestimated in assessing New York City's development. It allowed New York to make room for a succession of immigrant groups: The Germans, then the Irish, then the Jews and the Italians.

By the 1960's, the last of the new groups to migrate to the city, the blacks and Puerto Ricans, presented this system of accommodation with yet another test, which has become, in fact, its severest. Care must be taken not to combine blacks and Puerto Ricans, for they both have different origins and often different outlooks.

The basic difference between this new wave of in-migrants and those in the past is that, though both groups of newcomers come from other parts of the United States, both are largely non-white. In a sense, New York's problem has not been so different from that of other cities, many of which, in fact, have had a much higher proportion of blacks move into their city centers. Philadelphia, St. Louis, Detroit, and Washington, D.C. all notably have nearly double the proportion of blacks that New York City has.

But what makes New York City's situation different from all the rest is that it is a city not dominated by any one ethnic strain. It has always had a majority of minorities.

For a long period from the 1930's to the middle of the 1960's the Jewish group was automatically assumed to be on the side of the latest arrivals. In politics, the Jews and Italians formed many alliances which in effect ran the dominant Democratic Party, despite the fact that the Irish tended to hold most of the key positions of party leadership. The Jews were the one group who could be counted on to rally to the defense of the city's growing black population and to understand the problems encountered by the Puerto Ricans who began to move in from their island in the sun. The Jews were always assumed to be on the side of the underdog, no matter who that might be. They were believed to be the most liberal in outlook. Writing in Beyond The Melting Pot in 1963, Glazer and Moynihan said,

"The Jewish liberal voting pattern has been of great persistence. The transformation of Jews from a working-class group...to a middle-class group...has affected hardly at all their tendency to vote for liberal Democratic candidates... Upper-income Jews do not seem to be importantly differentiated from lower-income Jews in voting habits."*

But in 1968 a series of events took place which had a profound effect on the Jewish community in New York City. New York City has always known conflict, but of late it has become more intense and frequent. New York in the 1960's saw increased conflict in its universities, in its labor-management relations, in its welfare system, and, above all, in its schools. And it was the nature of this conflict, especially as it took place in the schools in 1968, which raised the subject of black-Jewish relations from the level of remote debate--among academics and intellectuals in the pages of Commentary, Israel Horizons, and the like--and made it a central issue of concern.

One of the most obvious changes in New York's mood during the late 1960's was the rise of militancy among its black leadership--a militancy which more and more involved a demand for local community control of local institutions Obviously, this development was important to the city as a whole, but it was especially important to substantial segments of New York's Jewish community. From the depression on, many Jews had found employment in the city's civil service in the very institutions, particularly the schools, where pressure was greatest for community control. By the late 1960's a majority of the teachers were Jewish and a majority of the students non-white. Unquestionably this situation prepared the way for conflict, making it probably, if not actually inevitable.

Although there were several areas where many blacks and Jews found themselves on opposite sides, education was at once the most noticeable and, by general agreement, the most important. Beginning with a boycott by black parents at Intermediate School (I.S.) 201 -- a brick, windowless Board of education showcase in East Harlem -- in September 1966. New York's school crisis moved through successive stages to become in the fall of 1968 the most debated dispute in New York City's history and certainly one of the bitterest. The development of this crisis provided the basic setting for the conflict between blacks and Jews.

---
*Cambridge, Mass.: MIT Press, 1963, p. 167

Even after a years time the atmosphere surrounding this crisis was too charged for anything approaching objectivity. From the outset the dispute centered around two experiments in local community control -- one made up of I.S. 201 and its feeder schools, the other in Brooklyn's Ocean Hill Brownsville School district.

The early days of these experiments, which went into operation in the fall of 1967, were tense, with the predominantly black parents and the predominantly Jewish teachers suspicious of each other's motives. And gradually, in late 1967 and early 1968, this tension gave way to open antagonism and became public. The first incident to attract widespread attention came at a memorial program in honor of Malcolm X at I.S. 201 on February 21, 1968. During the program several speakers denounced whites in unmistakably clear language. This was the first, but hardly the last, public incident in a dispute which produced considerable rancor from both sides.

In the spring of 1968, attention increasingly focused on events in the Ocean Hill-Brownsville district, which started its career as an experimental district more peacefully than I.S. 201 but became even more embattled. There, in late May the district administrator, Rhody McCoy, transferred 19 teachers out of the district. His action threw the school system into an uproar and prepared the way for the three acrimonious school strikes in the fall of 1968.

The story of the school strikes has been told and re-told, interpreted and re-interpreted. What is clear is that they came to have little to do with education and, as the disputes wore on, less and less to do with the usual stuff of labor negotiations and a great deal to do with race. Certainly there were issues at stake which concerned such topics as budgeting, job security, and due process. But the strong feelings of the major parties involved tended to obscure these issues as charges and countercharges of bigotry reverberated around the negotiations -- spokesmen for the teachers accusing Ocean Hill-Brownsville residents of anti-Semitism and local residents accusing the teachers of racial prejudice. And there is a good deal of evidence to support both points of view. For example, The Mayor's Special Committee on Racial and Religious Prejudice, headed by former State Supreme Court Judge Bernard Botein, issued a report (January 17, 1969) emphasizing the high degree of racial bitterness involved in the dispute. The report said,

> An appalling amount of racial prejudice -- black and white -- in New York City surfaced in and about the school controversy. Over and over again we found evidence of vicious anti-white attitudes on the part of some black people, and vicious anti-black attitudes on the part of some white people. The anti-white prejudice has a dangerous component of anti-Semitism.... On the other hand, anti-black bigotry tended to be expressed in more sophisticated and subtle fashion, often communicated privately and seldom reported, but nonetheless equally evil, corrosive, damaging, and deplorable.*

There was no question that some sort of confrontation had taken place between blacks and Jews. There was no question either that it had been bitter and intense -- that it had brought hostility, anger, and fear to the surface. The series of school strikes and confrontations surrounding the Ocean Hill-Brownsville experiment in school decentralization had a profound impact on all of the city, not just on the two major groups involved.

The shock waves from those events still seem to be reverberating through all of the boroughs. The school crisis made, if only temporarily, ardent pro-unionists out of Catholics in Staten Island and Queens who had increasingly voted conservative and whose sympathies were with the political philosophies of William Buckley and Barry Goldwater. It made the blacks wonder out loud if they had any friends left in the traditionally liberal strongholds of the Jewish community. It made Puerto Ricans look inward to wonder if they were going to be allied in the public mind with the blacks or whether they should seek out a traditional course of integration. It made Jews who had been raised in the tradition of self-sufficiency, excellence, and self-deprivation suddenly feel threatened by these new minority groups and made them re-examine their liberal tolerance of other, less fortunate minorities and their long-standing attachment to the ideas of the welfare system.

The city's system of accommodation appeared threatened as a new coalition of Jews and white Catholics began to emerge as a distinct possibility, not simply in the city's politics, but in the behavior of individuals in their daily lives. The basis

---

*Cited in Maurice Berube and Marilyn Gittell, eds., Confrontation at Ocean Hill-Brownsville (New York: Praeger Publishers, 1969) p. 174

for this coalition was essentially negative: fear and an active aversion to the thrust of the blacks.

The rhetoric of the school crisis had been harsh; its impact seemed profound. But, on the other side, there were strong ties, developed over the years, between blacks and Jews. These ties show themselves on many levels; in the prevalence of Old Testament figures in Negro spirituals; in the deaths of Michael Schwerner and Andrew Goodman, both Jews and both victims in the famous 1964 Mississippi civil rights murder case; and in the everyday life of New York City's politics.

The main questions which came out of the conflict between New York City's blacks and Jews are: How real a confrontation was it? How profound? How lasting?

The answers to these questions are important because of what they will say about the future relations of blacks and Jews in New York. They are also important because they will tell much about the future of New York's politics: whether it will continue to be liberal and whether its system of accommodation, its most basic characteristic, will survive.

Black-Jewish Relations in New York City

CHAPTER 1 TENSION AND CONFLICT

THE REALITY OF TENSION AND CONFLICT

Despite the traditional empathy between blacks and Jews in New York City, based largely on their both having suffered the hurt of discrimination, by mid-1969 there was general acknowledgment across the city that relations between the two groups had deteriorated (see Table 2).

Over-all, close to half the adult public in New York expressed the view that relations between Jews and blacks had worsened in the past few years. Scarcely more than one in ten thought they had improved. Puerto Ricans seemed least in touch with the conflict, with as much as a third of them unable to give a judgment, and another third saying they could see little or no change.

At the other extreme were the Jews, with a high 69 percent who saw a deterioration in black-Jewish relations. Only 5 percent saw an improvement. White Protestants perceived the situation as worse, by a 51-to-8-percent margin. White Catholics also were aware of a change for the worse by 43 to 13 percent.

Of all the groups, blacks appeared least impressed that there had been a real change. Although a plurality of 39 percent said relations had grown worse between the two groups, a relatively high 19 percent thought that relations had improved, and 34 percent saw little change. They were, then, the only group among whom a majority either saw no change or a shift for the better. Those blacks who thought relations had improved might believe that confrontation in the end would establish a new, more realistic and, possibly, more propitious relationship between the Jewish community and themselves. However, it would be a vast overdrawing of these data to make such a conclusion. Those blacks who saw little change might have felt that there always have been difficulties between the two groups. Certainly it can be said that blacks saw Jewish-black differences in far less alarming terms than the Jews.

TABLE 2

RELATIONS BETWEEN JEWS AND BLACKS IN PAST FEW YEARS

	Worse %	Better %	About Same %	Not Sure %
Total City	47	11	27	15
Jewish	69	5	19	7
Black	39	19	34	8
White Catholic	43	13	25	19
Puerto Rican	28	6	33	33
White Protestant	51	8	30	11
Manhattan	44	7	30	19
Bronx	44	20	27	9
Queens	48	10	30	12
Brooklyn	54	9	21	16
Richmond	68	12	12	8

Feelings Behind Views of Black-Jewish Relations

When asked on what they based their estimate, Jews gave the school dispute top billing, followed by "the mass media say it is worse."

Illustrative of the intensity felt among Jews was the comment of a 44-year-old college-educated executive from Manhattan who said: "Look what they did to the teachers. They made physical threats against the Jewish teachers. They singled them out. They are out to get the Jews, don't forget it." A Brooklyn businessman added: "People just don't get to be anti-Semites overnight. All they needed was a little match and what they really feel about Jews exploded but big." A Jewish housewife in Queens felt that the mass media fanned the hatred against the Jews: "The publicity during the strike was all against the Jews." Table 3 summarizes the reasoning of Jews on why relations with blacks had worsened.

When the blacks' views on relations between the two groups are examined, those who saw a decline also attributed it most of all to the school dispute.

TENSION AND CONFLICT 5

TABLE 3

FEELINGS BEHIND VIEWS ON BLACK-JEWISH RELATIONS: JEWS

	Total Jewish %
Why Worse	65
School strike	13
Mass media say it's worse	11
Jews are always scapegoats	8
Black militancy has alienated Jews	7
Violence and vandalism	6
Blacks becoming more hostile	4
Blacks feel Jews control ghettoes	4
Problem between whites and blacks	3
Blacks too demanding	3
Communists behind black protest	2
Have had bad personal experiences with blacks	2
There is more anti-Semitism	2
Why Better	5
Blacks can speak more freely	3
Both working for better life	2
No Change	19
Not Sure	11

Fourteen percent of the blacks volunteered that things have improved because "there is more dialogue now and even more cooperation". Illustrative of this thinking were the remarks of a skilled worker in Queens who earns $14,000 a year: "People today are learning to live and get along together, much better than before. Jews having suffered themselves know what it's like to have someone push you around and step on you." A cab driver in the Bronx said: "Many Jews whose ancestors have suffered as much as the black man have become more sympathetic toward blacks. Many Jews, I find, really want to help." A black college-educated professional said: "Blacks are getting to understand Jews more than they have before, and Jews are just beginning to understand that blacks want a straight shake for a change. It all has kind of cleared the air for the first time."

TABLE 4

FEELINGS BEHIND VIEWS ON JEWISH-BLACK
RELATIONS: BLACKS

	Total Blacks[a] %
Why Worse:	48
School dispute, decentralization	11
Blacks more aware of rights, demanding	9
Both more open now about their feelings, hostility	9
Jews rob, cheat blacks	5
From what mass media have said	3
Jews trying to keep blacks in place	3
Blacks tired of Jewish discrimination	2
Jewish backlash against black violence	2
Both inflexible, intolerant	2
Color differences emphasized more	2
Why Better:	18
More dialogues, cooperating more	14
Realizing they need each other to survive	4
Why Same:	29
Relations same, publicity just greater	20
Neither has progressed much	6
Jews still "haves," blacks "have nots"	3
Not Sure	12

[a] Adds to more than 100 percent as some respondents volunteered more than one answer.

This optimism was, at best, guarded, however. Blacks were most encouraged by their own sense of doing something about their plight. A black salesclerk in Bedford-Stuyvesant said: "The situation is clearer and better now. The black man is finally waking up and the Jews have to take notice." A black salesgirl in a Brooklyn department store added: "Things are better now because they are out in the open for all to see." A 24-year-old factory worker in Manhattan added: "Blacks are finally beginning to fight for jobs. The young people won't take it lying down anymore." A 55-year-old unemployed black from the Bronx said: "Well, we're still

TENSION AND CONFLICT

demonstrating and now we're really beginning to fight for our rights. You ain't seen nothin' yet." A 38-year-old stockroom clerk in Queens added: "Blacks are more vocal now on how they feel about being used in the world by Jewish merchants. We'll make the Jews understand what it's been like all this time." Table 4 summarizes the volunteered remarks of the black cross-section.

It is evident that both blacks and Jews saw the school dispute and the effects of the mass media as having contributed to a worsening in their relationship. Some Jews saw a change in black attitudes as contributing to the deterioration of the relation.

Blacks, for their part, tended to agree that blacks were changing, but they saw the net result of this new aggressiveness as producing beneficial results.

In addition to the comments on relations over the past few years, both blacks and Jews were asked what they felt were the reasons for differences between the two groups lately. How the blacks accounted for the differences is summarized in Table 5.

Other than agreeing with the blacks that the school trouble was a major part of the problem, the Jewish community had quite a different roster of reasons (see Table 6).

Although both groups pointed to the school strike as a central issue, in most of the other reasons cited each group tended to place blame on the other group.

Here are some illustrative statements: A 27-year-old Jewish college graduate in Queens put it this way: "The Negroes are jealous that the Jews have gotten ahead. All the Negroes can do is to demand that black studies be taught, in the hope that Jews won't be capable of teaching that subject." An unemployed 42-year-old black in Harlem chorused back: "That school decentralization aggravated the Jews, because they do not want the black man to have power. Well, man, the blacks are now determined to control their own lives." The assistant manager of a small retail store in Brooklyn who is Jewish said: "The militant Negroes are jealous that the Jew who is a minority can make it and get ahead and the Negro who is a minority hasn't got it to get ahead." A 39-year-old unemployed black man in Bedford-Stuyvesant answered: "The Jews have exploited us all these years. Now when we want to get ahead they don't like it. They like to work us out, but not have decent jobs." A Jewish foreman, aged 38, in Queens, who earns $13,000 a year, formulated it this way: "In the school situation, the black militants were looking for a fight and they

TABLE 5

REASONS FOR DIFFERENCES BETWEEN BLACKS
AND JEWS LATELY: BLACKS

	Total Blacks[a] %
School decentralization dispute and strike	20
Jews want to hold onto their position, blacks want to usurp it	9
Jews resent blacks trying to better themselves	9
Blacks beginning to compete with Jews for jobs, Jews threatened	6
Jews own stores with black workers, pay low wages	5
Jews exploit blacks financially	5
Just don't see eye to eye any more	5
Misunderstanding, different cultures	4
Jews have advantages, less discriminated against	4
Jews opposed to black-power methods	4
Slum landlords are Jews	3
The poor schools cause it	3
Housing, Jews don't want blacks in neighborhood	3
News media publicize the disputes	3
Jews own the ghetto stores where blacks shop	2
Wasn't aware of any differences	6
Not sure	19

[a] Adds to more than 100 percent as some respondents volunteered more than one answer.

picked on the Jewish school teachers who are among the few people who might have helped them." A black man in Brooklyn who makes $3,000 a year answered: "That Shanker, he's the one. He wants all the control, wants a following, wants it all for the Jews. See, because the Jews have suffered, they want the black people to suffer, too."

Thus, the language of the confrontation. Jews saw "black militants stirring up trouble," while blacks described it as "Jews are beginning to feel the heat of competition from the black man." Blacks saw it as "Jews want to hold onto their position," but Jews saw it as "blacks are envious of Jewish success." Blacks saw it as "Jews exploit blacks financially,

TABLE 6

REASONS FOR DIFFERENCES BETWEEN BLACKS AND JEWS LATELY: JEWS

	Total Jewish[a] %
School conflicts have increased hostilities	21
Blacks are envious, jealous of Jews	15
Blacks feel Jewish businessmen, landlords are exploiting them	12
Black militants stirring up trouble	11
Blacks need someone as a scapegoat	7
Too much attention to it in the press	6
Blacks feel Jews responsible for their lot	6
Blacks too demanding, too aggressive	5
Blacks trying to get things the easy way	4
Blacks fighting for rights as all minorities have	3
Outside agitators stirring it up	3
Blacks resent Jews in black neighborhoods	2
Blacks becoming more aware of what they want	2
Jews allowed opportunities blacks are denied	2
Struggle between black and white, not Jews	2
Not sure	13

[a] Adds to more than 100 percent as some respondents volunteered more than one reason.

own stores with black workers and pay low wages," but Jews saw it as "blacks need someone as a scapegoat and are too demanding and aggressive."

There was a minority among both groups who seemed to see how the other group feels and where sensitivities might have been offended. But as of mid-1969, both groups had tended to close ranks behind their own.

HOW BLACKS AND JEWS LOOK AT THE ESTABLISHMENT

The difference in perceptions between the black and Jewish communities is well illustrated in the estimates by both groups of where key parts of the establishment stood in the difficulties of 1968 (see Table 7).

It is significant that blacks felt that every institution had been more on the side of the Jews than on the side of the blacks. For their part, Jews believed that public authorities and politicians--the Mayor, the Welfare Department, white liberals, the city government, and political leaders--tended to be more on the side of the blacks than of the Jews. A large plurality of the blacks saw these authorities favoring neither side. All of the authorities obviously have been caught between the two adversary groups. However, it is well to point out that blacks saw whites generally, landlords, retail stores, the Police Department, white store owners, white real estate agents, the building trades unions, other labor unions, and white conservatives all as more on the Jewish than on the black side of the disputes.

The case of the police is an illustrative one. Though a plurality saw the police favoring neither side, blacks with opinions one way or the other tended to believe by a sizable margin that the police favored the Jewish side over their own. For their part, Jews tended to be interestingly divided over the role of the police, as Table 8 indicates.

In every borough but Manhattan a majority of the Jews said that the police were on neither side. In Manhattan 47 percent took this position. However, in Manhattan, the Bronx, and Queens, Jews expressing an opinion one way or the other tended to view the police as being on their side. But in Brooklyn there is a sharp shift. There, almost twice as many Jews saw the police as being pro-black as pro-Jewish. Besides Brooklyn Jews, those Jews upset about the police tended to be the less well educated, those over fifty, and those who follow the Orthodox faith. The young, the college-educated, and those not affiliated with any branch of the Jewish faith clearly believed the police were not pro-black during the Jewish-black confrontations.

THE ROOTS OF TENSION AND CONFLICT AMONG JEWS

This section deals with certain attitudes among white New Yorkers (especially Jews) which have contributed to tension and conflict. It focuses largely on the coming together of mounting public fear of crime and rising racial tensions--a singular mark of the 1960's, not only in New York but across

TABLE 7

BLACK AND JEWISH PERCEPTIONS OF ESTABLISHMENT SYMPATHIES

	Blacks				Jews			
	The Blacks' Side %	The Jews' Side %	Neither Side %	Not Sure %	The Blacks' Side %	The Jews' Side %	Neither Side %	Not Sure %
The Mayor	12	21	55	12	50	3	32	15
Welfare Department	11	25	44	20	49	3	28	20
White liberals	8	35	33	24	25	14	30	31
The city government	5	32	46	17	34	6	35	25
Political leaders	5	38	36	21	25	8	36	31
Whites generally	5	42	33	20	2	31	42	25
Landlords	4	35	38	23	3	34	42	21
Retail stores	3	41	37	19	3	23	53	21
Police Department	2	38	44	16	11	13	56	20
White store owners	2	47	31	20	3	30	47	20
White real estate agents	1	47	30	22	4	37	38	21
Building trades unions	1	45	31	23	4	13	42	41
Other labor unions	1	40	35	24	4	15	42	39
White conservatives	1	41	35	23	2	20	41	37

TABLE 8

JEWS' PERCEPTIONS OF POLICE DEPARTMENT SYMPATHIES

	Blacks' Side %	Jews' Side %	Neither Side %	Not Sure %
Total Jewish	11	13	56	20
Manhattan	2	21	47	30
Bronx	8	11	62	19
Queens	8	16	59	17
Brooklyn	17	9	55	19
Orthodox	18	8	56	18
Conservative	13	9	57	21
Reform	9	11	60	20
Non-affiliated	6	23	51	20
21-34	7	21	54	18
35-49	11	11	54	24
50+	13	8	59	20
8th grade	15	4	56	25
High school	14	10	54	22
College	6	19	56	19

the country. It also looks at some other indicators, particularly the pressures of living in New York City, and trends in neighborhoods. Partly due to extensive changes in the reporting of crime statistics and partly due to a real increase, public awareness and apprehension about crime has risen since the mid-1960's, and New York City has been no exception.

When queried on issues of personal concern, white New Yorkers displayed a high degree of concern over "going out on the street at night." Among both the non-Jewish white group and the special non-Jewish oversample group, this issue ranked only behind taxes as of concern. Among Jews, it ranked even ahead of taxes (see Table 18).

The figures in Table 9, taken from national surveys conducted in August 1964 and March 1968, give an indication of how much concern over violence and safety on the streets

TABLE 9

WORRY ABOUT VIOLENCE AND SAFETY ON STREETS: NATIONAL, 1964-1968

	More Worried 1964 %	More Worried 1968 %	Less Worried 1964 %	Less Worried 1968 %	Feel Same 1964 %	Feel Same 1968 %	Not Sure 1964 %	Not Sure 1968 %
Total National	50	52	5	4	42	42	3	2
Black	32	58	18	4	46	31	4	7
White								
Protestant	48	54	5	3	43	42	4	1
Catholic	56	52	4	5	39	42	1	1
Jewish	41	52	6	-	47	48	6	-

changed in the last half of the decade. They also help to put the study of New York City attitudes in some perspective. The answers New Yorkers gave to the same question (whether they were more worried, less worried, felt the same, or were not sure about violence and safety on the streets as compared to a year ago) are summarized in Table 10. The results show that New Yorkers in mid-1969 were, on the whole, substantially more worried than the nation in March of 1968.

Over-all, two out of every three New Yorkers said they are more worried about violence and safety on the streets now than they were a year ago. Among ethnic groups, Jews showed themselves more worried than the rest, while white Protestants showed least concern. Blacks, Puerto Ricans, and white Catholics came close to the city-wide average. Jewish women were significantly more worried than Jewish men. The borough breakdown is revealing: the residents of areas relatively lower in crime, Queens and Richmond, indicated more concern than did residents of Manhattan, Brooklyn, and the Bronx, the boroughs in which crime rates are higher.

Thus, as other studies of apprehension about crime have shown, New Yorkers in lower crime areas, while less threatened in reality, nonetheless have become even more apprehensive about crime than those living with it closer at hand. For example, a Harris survey of Baltimore opinion in the late 1960's found that more whites than blacks, and more low-crime-area residents than high-crime-area residents, feel crime is

TABLE 10

WORRY ABOUT VIOLENCE AND SAFETY ON STREETS:
CITY-WIDE

	More Worried %	Less Worried %	Feel Same %	Not Sure %
Total City	67	5	27	1
Jewish	79	2	18	1
Black	61	7	30	2
White Catholic	65	7	27	1
Puerto Rican	62	5	31	2
White Protestant	51	7	41	1
Jewish men	74	3	23	-
Jewish women	85	1	13	1
Manhattan	58	4	36	2
Bronx	69	13	18	-
Queens	72	1	26	1
Brooklyn	67	5	26	2
Richmond	80	-	20	-

a most serious problem. The phenomenon can be explained not by the obliviousness of high-crime-area residents but rather by the fact that in white, middle income, urban America by mid-1969, talk about imminent crime had nearly replaced the weather as the most common topic of conversation.

The racial overtones of concern about crime were immediately apparent when people were asked about their own fears of racial violence. The patterns of apprehension on racial outbreaks closely parallel those on worry about violence and safety in the street. Table 11 shows the results of a Harris survey conducted in March 1968, giving some sense of national opinion on fear of racial violence.

Table 12 summarizes New York City opinion on fear of racial violence in mid-1969. An identical number of New Yorkers--67 percent--expressed fear of racial violence and worry about safety in the streets, even though the city has been one of the few major metropolitan centers to avoid large-scale race riots. Again, Jews were most apprehensive,

TABLE 11

FEAR OF RACIAL VIOLENCE: NATIONAL, 1968

	Feel Uneasy %	Don't Feel It %	Not Sure %
Total Nationwide	48	47	5
White	46	50	4
Black	58	30	12
White Protestant	45	51	4
White Catholic	48	49	3
Jewish	63	32	5

TABLE 12

FEAR OF RACIAL VIOLENCE: CITY-WIDE

	Feel Uneasy %	Don't Feel It %	Not Sure %
Total City	67	28	5
Jewish	77	19	4
Black	55	39	6
White Catholic	67	29	4
Puerto Rican	73	18	9
White Protestant	59	38	3
Jewish men	72	25	3
Jewish women	84	13	3
Manhattan	64	29	7
Bronx	68	30	2
Queens	67	29	4
Brooklyn	69	25	6
Richmond	74	26	-

TABLE 13

OPINION BY AGE AND EDUCATION:
FEAR OF RACIAL VIOLENCE MAKES YOU UNEASY

	Uneasy %	Not Uneasy %	Not Sure %
Total Jewish	77	19	4
21-34	68	27	5
35-49	82	15	3
50 and over	81	16	3
8th grade	90	9	1
High school	82	14	4
College	69	27	4
Total Blacks	55	39	6
21-34	48	46	6
35-49	58	37	5
50 and over	62	30	8
8th grade	67	27	6
High school	53	40	7
College	45	52	3
Total Non-Jewish Whites	67	28	5
21-34	66	29	5
35-49	70	25	5
50 and over	65	29	6
No college	69	25	6
Some college	59	37	4

although Puerto Ricans ran a close second. Blacks were least worried about racial violence, along with white Protestants. Again, Jewish women were more frightened than Jewish men. And, again, Richmond, with almost no black population, led the way in expressing fears of racial outbreaks. The age and education divisions among the three key groups--Jews, non-Jewish whites, and blacks--is shown in Table 13.

TABLE 14

PRESSURES AND TENSIONS OF LIVING IN NEW YORK CITY: JEWS AND WHITES

	Increased %	Not Increased %	Not Sure %
Jewish	74	22	4
Non-Jewish whites	59	33	8
"Backlash" non-Jewish whites	72	23	5

The young of all groups tended to feel less uneasy than their elders. This is especially true of young Jews, 68 percent of whom were uneasy, while older Jews were considerably more concerned. The figures also show the college educated of all groups less fearful than the less educated.

A serious question must be raised about the connection between felt racial tensions and apprehension over crime. Much has been made about whites taking refuge in expressed fear over crime as a respectable way to vent their racial feelings. Some have charged that appeals to "law and order" and promises of "safety on the streets" are little more than veiled appeals to racism. The data of this study imply this possibility but do not prove it. Certainly, it is fair to conclude that fears of crime and racial hostilities are closely related, even though the two cannot be interchanged on a one-to-one basis.

When asked whether the pressures and tensions of living in New York City had increased or not increased, the Jewish community more than any other white group in the city believed they had increased. The regular sample of whites and the special oversample of whites who live in areas which voted 80 percent or more against the Civilian Review Board were asked how the pressures of living in the city compared with a few years ago; the answers are summarized in Table 14. Fifteen percent more Jews than non-Jewish whites reported increased pressures and tensions. Jews were slightly more apprehensive than even the special anti-Civilian Review Board oversample.

When the same white groups were asked about their own neighborhood and whether it was going down, getting better, or staying the same, about one third believed it to be going down, while about one half believed it to be staying the same (see Table 15).

TABLE 15

TREND OF OWN NEIGHBORHOOD: JEWS AND WHITES

	Going Down %	Getting Better %	Staying the Same %	Not Sure %
Jewish	35	10	49	6
Non-Jewish whites	30	12	50	8
Special non-Jewish white oversample	34	8	54	4

Again, a higher proportion of Jews than any other group believed their own neighborhood is deteriorating. The breakdown of the total Jewish group on how it rated its own living area is revealing, for it shows clearly where the tensions tended to be felt most deeply (see Table 16).

Jewish residents in Manhattan and Queens tended to be most satisfied with their neighborhoods. Almost a third of the Brooklyn Jews expressed dissatisfaction. But Bronx Jews clearly felt dissatisfaction the most. Most of these people live in neighborhoods which have had a recent influx of blacks and Puerto Ricans. The breakdown by segment of the Jewish faith is also revealing: Reform Jews were the most optimistic, Orthodox Jews were the least. Again, by age, younger Jews were well satisfied with their neighborhoods, but 45 percent of the older Jews expressed dissatisfaction. Educated Jews rated their neighborhoods high, but less well educated (and lower income) Jews expressed most dissatisfaction.

The same pattern is even more pronounced in the answers to the question dealing with the trend in own neighborhood; as shown in Table 17. Jews who live in the Bronx, who classify themselves as Orthodox, who are older and less well educated, all felt a decline in the neighborhoods in which they live. This sense of unease about their own home areas contributed to their sense of tension.

TABLE 16

RATING OF OWN NEIGHBORHOOD: JEWS

	Excellent/ Pretty Good %	Only Fair/ Poor %	Not Sure %
Total Jewish	67	33	-
Manhattan	78	21	1
Bronx	35	65	-
Queens	78	22	-
Brooklyn	67	32	1
Orthodox	56	43	1
Conservative	62	37	1
Reform	75	24	1
Non-affiliated	75	25	-
21-34	78	22	-
35-49	69	30	1
50+	55	45	-
8th grade	53	45	2
High school	62	37	1
College	73	26	1

In order to gain a kind of overview of the roots of tension and conflict in the city, the Jewish, non-Jewish white, and "backlash" samples were asked whether some generally prevalent concerns were problems to them and, if so, whether these problems were partly caused by racial tensions. The results are given in Table 18.

Almost without exception, Jews reported a higher concern with each problem that non-Jewish whites. In response to "going out on street at night," six in every ten Jews said they not only feel apprehension but also attribute this fear to racial tension. Less than five in ten whites in the special oversample area and four in ten non-Jewish whites shared the same feeling.

Roughly one in three Jews in New York City felt that racial tensions have affected the amount of taxes they pay, their problems in getting a good education for their children, and "having

TABLE 17

TREND OF OWN NEIGHBORHOOD: JEWS

	Going Down %	Getting Better %	Staying The Same %	Not Sure %
Total Jewish	35	10	49	6
Manhattan	26	31	34	9
Bronx	70	2	25	3
Queens	26	5	64	5
Brooklyn	29	6	59	6
Orthodox	47	2	42	9
Conservative	39	5	52	4
Reform	30	8	56	6
Non-affiliated	24	25	46	5
21-34	24	12	55	9
35-49	36	15	42	7
50+	43	4	48	5
8th grade	44	1	49	6
High school	40	6	48	6
College	28	16	50	6

their kids grow up in a decent, moral atmosphere." Both the special non-Jewish white oversample and the Jewish sample appeared more concerned about the impact of race on raising their children than did the non-Jewish white group.

When the Jewish group was looked at more closely in the dominant area of concern, "going out on street at night," sharp differences in the Jewish community emerged. These differences are summarized in Table 19.

The figures in the table reinforce the point that, in all age and educational categories, Jews showed themselves more concerned about going out on streets at night than non-Jewish whites. The data also indicate that the young and the college educated tend to be less concerned than their elders, among both the Jews and the non-Jewish whites.

Fear of violence clearly had become a dominant concern among a majroity of all New Yorkers by mid-1969. While

TABLE 18

PERSONAL PROBLEMS AND ATTRIBUTION TO RACE:
JEWS AND WHITES

	Jewish %	Non-Jewish Whites %	"Backlash" Non-Jewish Whites %
Going out on street at night			
Is a problem	74	55	65
Partly caused by racial tension	60	40	47
How much I pay in taxes			
Is a problem	73	64	76
Partly caused by racial tension	35	12	37
Getting good education for children			
Is a problem	53	42	49
Partly caused by racial tension	37	22	34
Having kids grow up in decent, moral atmosphere			
Is a problem	51	44	56
Partly caused by racial tensions	33	18	27
Feeling I am represented in city government			
Is a problem	41	42	45
Partly caused by racial tensions	18	14	21
Getting ahead on job			
Is a problem	27	27	33
Partly caused by racial tensions	8	6	6
Feeling good will from people around here			
Is a problem	20	18	10
Partly caused by racial tensions	10	5	2
Feeling like I am respected			
Is a problem	18	18	15
Partly caused by racial tensions	6	5	1

TABLE 19

GOING OUT ON STREET AT NIGHT: JEWS AND WHITES

	Big Problem %	Little Problem %	Racial Tension Is Cause %	Racial Tension Is Not Cause %	No Problem %	Not Sure %
Total Jewish	55	19	60	14	24	2
Manhattan	41	25	61	5	29	5
Bronx	64	11	56	19	25	-
Queens	48	22	45	25	30	-
Brooklyn	65	18	74	9	15	2
Orthodox	77	12	75	14	10	1
Conservative	63	15	65	13	21	1
Reform	55	21	63	13	24	-
Non-affiliated	25	28	37	14	41	2
21-34	44	23	52	15	33	-
35-49	51	21	56	16	26	2
50+	69	14	70	13	15	2
8th grade	80	6	78	8	14	-
High school	65	17	64	18	17	1
College	40	25	52	13	33	2
Total Non-Jewish Whites	37	18	44	16	43	2
21-34	36	16	38	15	46	1
35-49	38	19	47	15	41	2
50 and over	38	20	50	17	41	1
No college	41	21	47	18	37	2
Some college	26	10	33	9	63	1

TENSION AND CONFLICT 23

much of it was rooted in a felt rise in crime, definite and documentable overtones of racial tensions also were apparent. The most apprehensive group were the Jews, who traditionally have been viewed as most sympathetic to blacks among all white groups. Those parts of the Jewish community most fearful were the lower income, less affluent, Orthodox Jews, particularly in Brooklyn. Whether the physical fear sprang first from actual apprehension over crime or was a substitute for a growing concern over racial tensions is difficult to sort out. In fact, it matters little which came first. It can be reported that the two had become almost inextricably intertwined.

For the Jews, the roots of tension and conflict rested in this feeling of physical fear overladen with racial tensions and, to a lesser extent, in concern over the trend in their neighborhoods, as well as in such general concerns as paying taxes.

THE ROOTS OF TENSION AND CONFLICT AMONG BLACKS

If there were roots of tension in the Jewish community, then the lifelong frustration of being left out and discriminated against provided the impetus in the black community. The deep scars of three hundred years of second-class citizenship were most apparent in the alienation registered among blacks in New York City in response to the indexes listed in Table 20. Average alienation among blacks was almost twice as high as that among Jews and other whites, and 14 percentage points higher than was found among Puerto Ricans.

On the eight alienation items tested, blacks averaged 57 percent. Jews, white Catholics, and white Protestants all came in at roughly the 30 percent mark. The most sizable gaps appeared in two areas: "people with power take advantage of you," agreed to by 34 percent of the Jews but by a much higher 68 percent of the blacks; and "few people understand how it is to live like I live," agreed to by only 13 percent of the Jews but by 61 percent of the blacks.

In order to provide some sense of perspective, some results from national Harris surveys conducted in the summer of 1966, March 1968, and May 1969 are shown in Table 21.

New York blacks' alienation average--57 percent--is a good deal more than the national blacks' alienation average, which was 47 percent in the May 1969 national survey. Even the 57 percent figure for alienation among New York blacks

TABLE 20

ALIENATION: CITY-WIDE

	Total City %	Jewish %	Black %	White Catholic %	Puerto Rican %	White Protestant %
Rich get richer, poor get poorer	69	63	85	64	66	68
People running city don't care what happens to people like me	48	44	61	46	53	40
What I think doesn't count much	40	35	52	39	42	36
People with power take advantage of you	42	34	68	30	53	35
When you try to be nice to people in other groups, you get no thanks for it	29	26	52	19	35	14
I feel left out of things	26	15	45	21	41	15
Few people understand how it is to live like I live	26	13	61	13	37	17
Important things in city don't affect my life	15	9	30	10	20	6
Average alienation	37	30	57	30	43	29

TABLE 21

ALIENATION: NATIONAL

	Total Public 1966 %	1968 %	1969 %	Blacks 1966 %	1968 %	1969 %
Rich get richer, poor get poorer	48	53	57	49	55	61
What I think doesn't count much	39	50	38	40	57	47
People in power don't care much about us	28	41	35	32	50	46
Other people get lucky breaks	19	22	21	35	40	43
Important events in world don't affect me	18	28	22	12	40	27
Few people understand how I live	18	28	25	32	61	56

TABLE 22

ALIENATION: BLACKS, CITY-WIDE

	Total Blacks %	Income Under $3,000 %	Income $3,000 to $6,999 %	Income $7,000+ %	On Welfare %
Rich get richer, poor get poorer					
Agree	85	87	87	82	89
Disagree	12	10	10	15	9
Not sure	3	3	3	3	2
People who have power are out to take advantage of you					
Agree	68	77	72	55	78
Disagree	21	15	17	31	12
Not sure	11	8	11	14	10
People running city don't care what happens to people like me					
Agree	61	72	64	47	72
Disagree	30	19	26	45	21
Not sure	9	9	10	8	7
Few people understand how it is to live like I live					
Agree	61	77	64	48	73
Disagree	30	15	27	43	19
Not sure	9	8	9	9	8
What I think doesn't count very much					
Agree	52	67	55	38	66
Disagree	42	27	38	58	30
Not sure	6	6	7	4	4
When you try to be nice to people in other groups you get no thanks for it					
Agree	52	70	53	38	65
Disagree	34	21	31	48	21
Not sure	14	9	16	14	14
I feel left out of things					
Agree	45	63	51	30	58
Disagree	49	31	42	66	34
Not sure	6	6	7	4	8
Important things in city don't affect my life					
Agree	30	46	34	19	42
Disagree	65	48	61	78	54
Not sure	5	6	5	3	4
Average Alienation	57	70	60	45	68

understates the depths of despair experienced by key sectors of the black community. When the blacks were looked at by income groups and by whether they were on welfare or not, alienation rose to 68 percent for those on welfare and 70 percent for all those earning under $3,000 annually (see Table 22).

Alienation among blacks in New York was appreciably higher than among blacks nationwide. The 1969 national survey, using a similar alienation scale, showed that 47 percent qualify as "alienated." Among low-income blacks nationally, alienation rose to 61 percent, significantly below the 70 percent mark recorded in New York City in this study.

Some of the blacks' alienation centered on material items-- the felt hurt of the blacks was physical in the deprivation they felt in their housing, education, and job opportunities. But the psychological impact was even greater. Given the level of alienation from dominant white society, one might wonder how New York City has escaped major racial conflagration in recent years. Minimally, the potential for confrontation among blacks in this city was plain to see as measured by the extent of their alienation.

CHAPTER **2** A COMMON BOND: PERCEPTIONS OF DISCRIMINATION

In the past, most young blacks and most young Jews took identification of their groups as minorities for granted. A part of both the black and Jewish heritages has been to learn at an early age that "you belong to a minority." It has been implicit in this awareness that a young person must be prepared to suffer discrimination. Implicit, too, has been the assumption that people from other groups will not be nearly as willing to admit that discrimination exists and, in fact, will practice it.

DISCRIMINATION AGAINST JEWS

This pattern is indeed borne out in the case of how Jewish people and the rest of New York viewed discrimination against Jews in the city. By 45 to 44 percent, Jews in New York City believed they are discriminated against. By a clear 52 to 29 percent, the city as a whole did not think Jews are discriminated against. The breakdown by key groups and by boroughs of the city is given in Table 23.

There was little doubt in the minds of most white Catholics (62 percent to 18 percent), Puerto Ricans (53 percent to 9 percent), or white Protestants (67 percent to 15 percent) that Jews in the city are not discriminated against. People living in Richmond and Queens were least convinced of anti-Jewish discrimination. Only in Manhattan could one find less than a majority who denied this discrimination.

In all of the city, there was only one exception to this pattern--blacks. Blacks tended to see discrimination against Jews almost identically as Jews themselves perceived it: 42 percent to 40 percent said that there is discrimination against Jews. The pattern among blacks by borough, shown in Table 24, has significance.

TABLE 23

PERCEPTIONS OF DISCRIMINATION AGAINST JEWS
IN CITY: BY GROUP AND BOROUGH

	Discrimination %	No Discrimination %	Not Sure %
Total City	29	52	19
Jewish	45	44	11
Black	42	40	18
White Catholic	18	62	20
Puerto Rican	9	53	38
White Protestant	15	67	18
Manhattan	30	43	27
Bronx	31	56	13
Queens	26	59	15
Brooklyn	29	52	19
Richmond	25	75	--

TABLE 24

PERCEPTIONS OF DISCRIMINATION AGAINST JEWS
IN CITY: BLACKS

	Discrimination %	No Discrimination %	Not Sure %
Total Blacks	42	40	18
Manhattan	47	33	20
Bronx	53	35	12
Queens	43	49	8
Brooklyn	34	46	20

TABLE 25

PERCEPTIONS OF DISCRIMINATION AGAINST JEWS IN CITY: JEWS

	Discrimination %	No Discrimination %	Not Sure %
Total Jewish	45	44	11
21-34	41	48	11
35-49	49	40	11
50+	46	43	11
Under $10,000	53	37	10
$10,000-$15,000	41	47	12
Over $15,000	36	54	10
8th grade	65	26	9
High school	44	44	12
College	39	49	12

Blacks in the Bronx were most convinced (53 to 35 percent) that Jews were discriminated against. A similar pattern is evident among Manhattan blacks. But in Queens and Brooklyn, the results reversed themselves: blacks in these boroughs, especially Brooklyn, tended to feel Jews are not discriminated against.

Within the Jewish community itself, there was wide difference in perception of anti-Jewish discrimination, as Table 25 shows.

The most affluent Jews, those earning over $15,000 and who have had some college education, clearly tended to deny that discrimination against Jews existed. By a margin of 48-41 percent, Jews under 35 years of age also tended to believe their co-religionists are not victims of discrimination. By contrast, older, less affluent, and less well educated Jews believed they are discriminated against.

A similar pattern emerges when Jews were asked to give their estimate on whether or not anti-Jewish feeling is on the rise, diminishing or not changing in the city; the responses are shown in Table 26.

TABLE 26

ESTIMATE OF ANTI-JEWISH FEELING IN CITY: JEWS

	On Rise %	Diminishing %	About Same %	Not Sure %
Total Jewish	46	6	39	9
Manhattan	45	5	32	18
Bronx	38	4	47	11
Queens	35	7	49	9
Brooklyn	58	5	30	7
Orthodox	56	3	32	9
Conservative	52	5	34	9
Reform	40	7	41	12
Non-affiliated	36	9	49	6
21-34	41	6	44	9
35-49	47	7	36	10
50+	49	5	35	11
8th grade	52	2	30	16
High school	49	5	38	8
College	40	7	41	12

A larger proportion of Brooklyn Jews perceived rising anti-Semitism than those in the other boroughs. Orthodox Jews felt most strongly this way, followed by Conservative Jews, with Reform and non-affiliated Jews feeling least of all that anti-Jewish sentiment is on the rise. Again, older Jews tended to see an increase in anti-Jewish feeling more than younger Jews. Those with less education reported they could observe an increase much more than did the college educated.

It is now apparent that those Jews who felt most put upon by anti-Semitic sentiment--those who live in Brooklyn, those who practice Orthodox Judaism, older and less well educated Jews--also tended to feel most concerned about racial violence, and saw racial overtones in threats to their own safety.

The comments volunteered by Jews when asked why they estimated anti-Semitism was on the rise or not showed some association of anti-Jewish feeling with the blacks, as Table 27 shows.

TABLE 27

FEELINGS BEHIND ESTIMATE OF ANTI-JEWISH FEELING: JEWS

	Total Jewish [a] %
Why on Rise	57
Blacks talk it, put out literature	13
Newspapers magnify it	12
Due to school conflict	8
Burning of synagogues	6
Usual anti-minority prejudice	6
People jealous of Jewish success	4
More tension, can feel it	3
Blacks lashing out at all minorities	3
Jews do discriminate	1
Due to Israeli-Arab conflict	1
Why Diminishing	7
Still there, but going down	4
Cooling down since school strike	3
Why Same	39
Always has been anti-Semitism	22
Just more visible	17
Not Sure	6

[a] Adds to more than 100 percent as some respondents volunteered more than one response.

The most frequently volunteered reasons for rising anti-Semitism were "blacks talk it, put out literature," "newspapers magnify it," "the school conflict," "blacks lashing out at all minorities." Illustrative was a statement by a 61-year-old Jewish clerk in Brooklyn, who said: "Those Negroes are ignorant people. They can be influenced in any direction. Being against the Jews is in the limelight now. Bad people are getting them all stirred up." A Brooklyn Jewish shopkeeper added: "I know it is so because I read the stories in the newspaper how the Negroes are out to get the Jews. The teachers' strike was all racial, aimed at the Jews. There was a terrible lot of dirt thrown at the Jews." A retired 65-year-old man who lives on the Lower East Side of Manhattan said: "I've heard about the hate pamphlets put out among the Negroes, especially among the younger ones who eat that stuff up."

Not all of the believed rise was attributed to blacks. The wife of a professional who lives in Queens said: "Catholics have always hated us. We are still blamed for the crucifixion. It has always been that way. We killed Christ, so we're no good. Terrible thing." A skilled laborer in Brooklyn, earning over $15,000, diagnosed it this way: "Well, they still hold those Bund meetings in Yorkville and then they spread their literature all over the city."

The study attempted to find out if non-Jews were able to project how it might feel to be discriminated against as a Jew. All of the volunteered answers by blacks are summarized in Table 28.

The percentage of blacks who expressed sympathy for Jews who are discriminated against totals 43 percent; this is close to the 42 percent who perceived discrimination against Jews (as tabulated in Table 24) though the two measures are not strictly comparable. Easily the most frequent reaction was "feel much the same as black people." Illustrative was an unskilled black laborer in Brooklyn, age 38, who said: "To be discriminated against is a terrible feeling. It makes you sick inside. Jews feel it just the same as we do." A black clerical worker in Manhattan added: "Discrimination hurts any man whether he is black or white or Jew. Maybe that is why the Jews respect any man no matter who."

But a number of the blacks added an important qualification: Jews may suffer from discrimination, but they don't "feel it as much, because they have so many other advantages going for them." A 21-year-old black key punch operator in Manhattan observed: "It makes them more determined to become a winner and to prove themselves and to work harder and to have people look up to them." A black social worker in Brooklyn said: "I'm sure they feel the same as a black man, but they don't really care, because they stick so close together and they have all the money and they don't need anyone else." A black subway worker added: "It just makes them determined all the more to go out and make more money."

Reaction among the non-Jewish white community to the same question was at best mixed, as Table 29 indicates.

TABLE 28

PERCEPTIONS OF JEWS' FEELINGS ABOUT DISCRIMINATION: BLACKS

	Total Blacks[a] %
Feel the same as a black person	22
Don't feel it so much because they have advantages	11
It feels bad	10
The same as anyone else who is discriminated against	7
Makes them try harder to succeed	4
Doesn't hurt them any	3
Same as for blacks, but not as bad	2
Discourages them, takes away dignity and pride	2
Will cause them to strike out and discriminate	2
Don't know how it feels to them	9
They aren't discriminated against	9
Not sure	28

[a] Adds to more than 100 percent as some respondents volunteered more than one answer.

A minority of the non-Jewish whites responded with some empathy. Illustrative was this statement by an Irish union member from Queens: "It must make them very bitter. After all, it's a deep hurt." A young Catholic secretary from Manhattan said: "you wouldn't like it at all, because that feeling exists only because of your religion." A grocery store manager in Brooklyn said: "It makes any individual discriminated against feel sorry for himself. But in the Jews' case, they just work all the harder. I see it all the time."

But most of the non-Jewish whites, coming to seven in every ten, could not bring themselves to empathize with Jews who are discriminated against. An Italian hairdresser in Manhattan said: "I think they are paranoids. As a group, they want to see themselves as a bunch of martyrs." A young Puerto Rican girl who works as a clerk in the Bronx made this observation: "No, there is no discrimination against them, because New York is a Jewish town." A foreman in Queens, earning close to $15,000, added: "They want you to think they are discriminated against so they can justify themselves in giving the rest of us a harder time."

TABLE 29

PERCEPTIONS OF JEWS' FEELINGS OF DISCRIMINATION: NON-JEWISH WHITES

	Total Non-Jewish Whites %
Must be miserable, depressing	13
Makes them aggressive, try harder	6
Makes them feel inferior	5
Only a little prejudice against them	4
Makes them angry	3
Have wealth, power--why worry?	3
Increases their unity	2
Makes them bitter and prejudiced	2
No idea	13
No worse than any others	8
Jews not discriminated against	12
Not sure	37

 To charge that there is discrimination against Jews in New York City is a controversial claim. The Jews themselves were split on the issue, but a razor-thin plurality believed they are victims of prejudice, and Jews by a substantial margin, 46-6 percent, saw anti-Jewish feeling rising as opposed to going down. Among non-Jewish whites, there were distinct signs that raising the charge of discrimination against Jews evoked from many some anti-Jewish feeling.
 Significantly, only the blacks tended to share the Jews' feelings about discrimination.

TABLE 30

PERCEPTIONS OF DISCRIMINATION AGAINST BLACKS IN CITY: BY GROUP AND BOROUGH

	Discrimination %	No Discrimination %	Not Sure %
Total City	61	30	9
Jewish	58	34	8
Black	86	9	5
White Catholic	42	48	10
Puerto Rican	66	22	12
White Protestant	59	32	9
Manhattan	77	17	6
Bronx	58	35	7
Queens	57	33	10
Brooklyn	50	38	12
Richmond	64	30	6

TABLE 31

PERCEPTIONS OF DISCRIMINATION AGAINST BLACKS IN CITY: WHITE CATHOLICS

	Discrimination %	No Discrimination %	Not Sure %
Total White Catholics	42	48	10
21-34	52	40	8
35-49	48	48	4
50 and over	31	58	11
Italian	40	53	7
Irish	48	41	11
No college	37	52	11
College	64	32	4

TABLE 32

PERCEPTIONS OF DISCRIMINATION AGAINST BLACKS IN CITY: JEWS

	Discrimination %	No Discrimination %	Not Sure %
Total Jewish	58	34	8
Manhattan	77	17	6
Bronx	57	38	5
Queens	64	32	4
Brooklyn	42	42	16
Orthodox	48	42	10
Conservative	48	43	9
Reform	57	34	9
Non-affiliated	79	17	4
21-34	75	21	4
35-49	65	27	8
50+	38	49	13
Under $10,000	51	37	12
$10,000-$15,000	64	28	8
$15,000 and over	63	32	5
8th grade	31	53	16
High school	48	43	9
College	74	20	6

DISCRIMINATION AGAINST BLACKS

If the Jews encounter some difficulty in arousing sympathy on the score of discrimination in New York, blacks by and large do not, as Table 30 shows.

By a margin of 61 to 30 percent--two to one--most New Yorkers felt blacks are discriminated against. As might be expected, Negroes themselves felt most strongly about it, with 86 percent seeing discrimination. But sizable majorities of Jews, Puerto Ricans and white Protestants also shared this view.

PERCEPTIONS OF DISCRIMINATION

The one group which demurred in this estimate about anti-black discrimination was white Catholics, who also felt most strongly that Jews are not discriminated against. Over-all, in the borough-by-borough breakdown, Manhattan was overwhelmingly convinced that anti-black prejudice exists, while only half of Brooklyn had that view. The breakdown of the results among white Catholics shown in Table 31 reveals significant divisions. All white Catholics were by no means uniform in their estimate. In fact, those under 35 and those with some college education showed majorities who felt there is discrimination against blacks. The Irish tended to see more anti-black prejudice than was the case among Italians. In the end, however, with the Catholics, the weight of opinion among older people, the Italians, and the less affluent (no college) have the plurality to "blacks are not discriminated against" in New York City. Among the Jewish community, similar wide differences could also be observed, as Table 32 shows.

Manhattan and Queens Jews were most agreed that anti-black discrimination does exist. But Brooklyn Jews were split down the middle. Orthodox and Conservative Jews were less convinced, while Reform Jews clearly believed it is there. Non-affiliated Jews also felt it was there more than any others.

But the sharpest differences among the Jews in their estimate of anti-black discrimination can be seen when age, income, and educational cuts are examined. Young Jews under 35 were overwhelmingly convinced that discrimination against blacks exists in the city, but those over 50 were not. A comparable difference exists between the college-educated, who were convinced by better than three to one that there is discrimination, compared with those who did not go beyond the eighth grade, a majority of whom were thoroughly convinced it is not real. The pattern by income parallels that for education; the higher the income of a Jewish family, the higher the awareness of anti-black discrimination. (See Table 33.)

Comparing Jews' and non-Jewish whites' perceptions of discrimination against blacks (Table 32 and 33), the pattern revealed is one that has appeared to some extent in other responses already reported: age and educational background can be as important as ethnic ties.

Within both the white Catholic and Jewish groups, sharp differences exist by age and education. The young and the educated tended to see far more discrimination against blacks. This finding suggests the possibility that an approach toward ameliorating racial relations in New York might be through

TABLE 33

PERCEPTIONS OF DISCRIMINATION AGAINST BLACKS IN CITY: NON-JEWISH WHITES

	Discrimination %	No Discrimination %	Not Sure %
Total Jewish	58	34	8
21-34	75	21	4
35-49	65	27	8
50 and over	38	49	13
8th grade	31	53	16
High school	48	43	9
College	74	20	6
Total Non-Jewish White	54	36	10
21-34	60	28	12
35-49	56	36	8
50 and over	39	48	13
No college	48	40	12
Some college	72	24	4

the young and the better educated working together, regardless of religion.

To test this possibility further, the special group of whites who live in the areas which voted 80 percent or more against the Civilian Review Board must be examined (see Table 34). Over-all, this special group felt, by 58 to 34 percent, that blacks are not discriminated against. The pattern among Italian and Irish in the group parallels that for white Catholics as a whole, with the Italian group more convinced that discrimination against blacks does not exist.

But the most dramatic differences again can be found by age and educational difference. The young tended more than the others to see discrimination against blacks, and the educated more than the less well educated saw it.

Significantly, the businessmen who live in these special areas tended, by 50 to 41 percent, to see discrimination against blacks. White collar, skilled labor, and unskilled

PERCEPTIONS OF DISCRIMINATION

TABLE 34

PERCEPTIONS OF DISCRIMINATION AGAINST BLACKS IN CITY: "BACKLASH" WHITES

	Discrimination %	No Discrimination %	Not Sure %
Total Special Group	34	58	8
Italian	28	65	7
Irish	45	49	6
21-34	46	47	7
35-49	27	68	5
50 and over	26	60	14
No college	31	60	9
Some college	47	46	7
Businessmen	50	41	9
White collar	28	65	7
Skilled labor	26	64	10
Unskilled labor	31	61	8

labor groups, by contrast, all by two to one or better, denied its existence.

A final test of the hypothesis that there may be bonds between the young and the educated which could be stronger than ethnic group ties is to examine the responses to the same question by the black cross-section, as shown in Table 35.

It is immediately apparent that large majorities of all segments of the black community were convinced that discrimination against them is a reality. However, the differences by age (under and over 50) and by income and by education are clearly there. The young blacks, the better educated, and the more affluent all tended to see more discrimination.

There is, then, an undeniable pattern which runs deep, quite independently of race and religion. The young, the educated, the affluent all tended to see more discrimination against blacks, whether they are white Catholics, Jews, whites who live in areas which voted 80 percent or more against the Civilian Review Board, or, indeed, are black themselves.

TABLE 35

PERCEPTIONS OF DISCRIMINATION AGAINST BLACKS IN CITY: BLACKS

	Discrimination %	No Discrimination %	Not Sure %
Total Negroes	86	9	5
Manhattan	86	10	4
Bronx	88	8	4
Queens	92	5	3
Brooklyn	83	11	6
21-34	88	9	3
35-49	88	8	4
50+	79	12	9
8th grade	77	14	9
High school	88	8	4
College	91	8	1
Under $3,000	77	19	4
$3,000-$6,999	88	7	5
$7,000+	90	7	3
On welfare	80	14	6
Men	88	9	3
Women	85	9	6

The implication of this result is that there is a basis for broad-scale community efforts at reconciliation among the young, the educated, and the affluent. The groups most difficult to bring together would be older people, those with less education, the less affluent, particularly among the Jews who live in Brooklyn, and a majority of the Italian group.

Both the Jews and the blacks tended to see more discrimination against both their groups than white Catholics do. In other words, white Catholics, the largest group in New York City, denied by a sizable majority that either blacks or Jews are discriminated against in the city. By contrast, the largest

PERCEPTIONS OF DISCRIMINATION 41

body of opinion among both Jews and blacks saw discrimination against both groups. This suggests less that Catholics are bigoted than that Jews and blacks may have more in common than has seemed apparent lately in New York City.

As part of the questionnaire employed in this study, both blacks and Jews were read a statement: "The real bigots like nothing better than to see Jews and blacks at each other's throats." They were asked if they tended to agree or disagree. By 85 to 5 percent, Jews agreed, as did blacks by 77 to 7 percent.

Clearly, however, in the heat of controversy in 1968 and in 1969, the prospect of an outside force which could have stronger feelings against both Jews and blacks than either hold for the other was not foremost on the minds of either embattled group.

CHAPTER 3   HOW BLACKS ARE PERCEIVED

Confrontation consists of at least two essential elements: a sense that the target group cannot be approached through any other means and an issue on which neither side will yield. Some of the specific situations in New York City which have exacerbated black-Jewish relations are dealt with in another chapter.

But the events themselves cannot be properly understood unless a rather extensive examination is made of how the minorities in New York view the blacks and the Jews as groups. The preconceptions, as well as the post-conceptions, are crucial, both in trying to piece together what has happened and, even more important, in charting courses for alleviation of tensions in the period ahead.

In many ways, the decade of the 1960's began with a firm assumption that the heartland of discrimination and prejudice in America was the eleven southern states, that it was there that the crisis between black and white had to be resolved. The decade ended with almost daily events presenting clear evidence that the future of race relations in this country will be written in the central cities, the urban core.

The reasons are apparent upon analysis. Easily the fastest growth in the black population can be found in metropolitan America. At the end of the 1960's it was estimated that 45 percent of the blacks lived in the South, 15 percent in the ring of border states just outside the South. The remaining 40 percent inhabited the metropolitan areas of the North. And within each northern metropolis, blacks almost inevitably will be found populating the central city core, the inner city.

In New York City at the end of the decade, it was estimated that 400,000 out of 2,000,000 families or household units were black. What these blacks want as well as how well nonblacks understand what they want will be decisive in whether New York survives or explodes.

Both blacks and the rest of the adult population were asked what they think blacks want in the city; the results are shown in Table 36.

TABLE 36

CITY-WIDE OPINION: WHAT BLACKS WANT IN NEW YORK

	Total City %	Jewish %	Black %	White Catholic %	Puerto Rican %	White Protestant %
To Achieve Full Equality						
Want	85	84	97	80	79	85
Don't want	7	7	1	11	8	7
Not sure	8	9	2	9	13	8
To Find Own Identity As Blacks						
Want	78	81	85	73	69	80
Don't want	8	5	10	10	7	6
Not sure	14	14	5	17	24	14
To Achieve Complete Integration with Whites						
Want	58	44	74	56	65	58
Don't want	23	31	17	26	10	24
Not sure	19	25	9	18	25	18
To Keep Pressure on Whites						
Want	57	70	52	51	52	58
Don't want	26	17	38	27	20	28
Not sure	17	13	10	22	28	14
To Have Separate but Equal Rights						
Want	40	45	40	42	31	29
Don't want	35	29	50	28	30	45
Not sure	25	26	10	30	39	26
To Tear Down White Society						
Want	32	45	20	34	31	25
Don't want	47	34	69	43	38	52
Not sure	21	21	11	23	31	23

On many key objectives, the entire community of New York City, including blacks, were in substantial agreement. Well over eight in ten believed blacks want "full equality." Among blacks themselves, this objective rose to 97 percent, close to unanimity. Over three in four agreed that "blacks want to find their own identity as blacks." Among blacks themselves, 85 percent felt this way, but other groups were not far below this percentage in their assessment of this black objective.

By the same token, there was substantial doubt that blacks want "separate but equal rights." The results indicate that 40 percent of all blacks in New York favored the "separate but equal" idea, but 50 percent rejected it. White Protestants were most emphatic in believing that blacks do not want this objective (45 to 29 percent). But the Jewish and white Catholic groups were less convinced. By 45 to 29 percent, Jews felt blacks do want it, and by 42 to 28 percent, white Catholics shared this view. At best, it can be concluded that the "separate but equal" approach has some support among blacks and that some whites believe blacks want a separate society. These views do not achieve a majority among either blacks or whites. (Separatism is a sensitive subject in race relations today. For, as often happens in polarized situations, extremists in both camps can come to the same conclusions, even if for opposite reasons. Thus, some black militants advocate a separate black society so that blacks can find their full identity without the encumbrances of white dominance. For years, of course, white racists have advocated the "separate but equal" notion for blacks.)

The opposite concept, "complete integration with whites", reveals the first sharp division between blacks and Jews. By 74 to 17 percent, blacks believed strongly in integration as a major goal. Yet the Jewish community was convinced that blacks wanted it by only a relatively narrow 44 to 31 percent. Puerto Ricans believed it by 65 to 10 percent, white Protestants by 58 to 24 percent, and white Catholics by 56 to 26 percent.

Two areas of tactics were probed: wanting to "keep pressure on whites" and wanting to "tear down white society." A majority of all groups said blacks want to keep pressure on white society as a goal, including a 52 to 38 percent margin among the blacks themselves. However, it must be noted that Jews were convinced blacks want to "keep the pressure on" by a much higher margin, 70-17 percent.

By contrast, only a minority of all groups believed that blacks want to "tear down white society." Significantly, howeve

HOW BLACKS ARE PERCEIVED 45

the group most opposed to this stereotype were the blacks themselves, who rejected this idea by 69 to 20 percent. Puerto Ricans and white Catholics did not believe it by 38-31 percent and 43-34 percent, respectively. White Protestants did not believe it by a more substantial 52 to 25 percent. But a plurality of Jews did believe it, by 45 to 34 percent. The only group which appeared more worried about blacks "tearing down white society" in New York City in mid-1969 was the special group of whites who live in areas which voted 80 percent or more against the Civilian Review Board in 1966. By 47-29 percent, they said this is a prime black objective.

The polarization between the black and Jewish communities is immediately apparent in these results. Jews tended to believe that blacks are off on a tack of wanting to build their own separate society by tactics of mounting pressure on whites and even by "tearing down white society." The divisions among blacks did not accord with what Jews thought they were on these issues. Blacks showed themselves far more committed to integration than Jews believed and far less intent on pressuring white society, and particularly "tearing it down," than Jews feared.

A finding of this study, therefore, must be stated: the Jewish group in New York City has developed some serious misapprehensions about the motives and intent of the black community.

"TEARING DOWN WHITE SOCIETY"

The charge of "tearing down white society" is so serious that it deserves a more detailed examination. In these results some of the outlines of future confrontations may be found. First, the breakdown among blacks, which shows where the pressures for "tearing down white society" come from (see Table 37). Only among three black groups did 30 percent say they want to "tear down white society"--those who have never been to high school, those earning under $3,000 a year, and those on welfare. Significantly, however, even among these groups, it must be noted that a majority still rejected this destructive approach.

The pattern among the key Italian and Irish groups within the white Catholic segment is shown in Table 38.

The results of this breakdown show that Catholics of Irish origin divided about as the overall peer group did, except that

TABLE 37

BLACKS WANT TO TEAR DOWN WHITE SOCIETY:
BLACK OPINION

	Want %	Don't Want %	Not Sure %
Total Blacks	20	69	11
Manhattan	16	72	12
Bronx	26	68	6
Queens	15	76	9
Brooklyn	23	64	13
21-34	22	66	12
35-49	22	66	12
50+	14	77	9
8th grade	31	54	15
High school	17	72	11
College	19	72	9
Under $3,000	36	53	11
$3,000-$6,999	18	70	12
$7,000+	15	74	11
On welfare	31	56	13
Men	22	67	11
Women	18	70	12

TABLE 38

BLACKS WANT TO TEAR DOWN WHITE SOCIETY:
WHITE CATHOLIC OPINION

	Want %	Don't Want %	Not Sure %
Total White Catholics	34	43	23
Italian	44	34	22
Irish	42	51	7

HOW BLACKS ARE PERCEIVED 47

TABLE 39

BLACKS WANT TO TEAR DOWN WHITE SOCIETY:
"BACKLASH" WHITE OPINION

	Want %	Don't Want %	Not Sure %
Total Non-Jewish White "Backlash"	47	29	24
Catholic	50	29	21
Non-Catholic	36	30	34
Italian	49	22	29
Irish	46	29	25
21-34	44	33	23
35-49	52	29	19
50+	45	25	30
No college	52	25	23
Some college	25	48	27
Belong to union	50	27	23
Skilled labor	51	24	25
Unskilled labor	60	21	19

the Irish tended to be more certain than the Italian group, one way or the other, in their views about whether blacks do want to tear down white society. However, the Italian group reversed the pattern, a 44 percent plurality believing this to be a black objective. This difference between the Italian and Irish communities is evident throughout this study, the former expressing more apprehension about the black thrust in the city.

The responses of the special sample of non-Jewish whites in the areas which voted 80 percent or more against the Civilian Review Board sheds further light on the possibilities of future polarization (see Table 39).

It is evident immediately from these results that the Catholics more than the non-Catholics, the Italians more than the Irish, the non-college-educated more than the college-educated, and the unskilled labor segment more than the skilled labor segment of this special "backlash" group were convinced that blacks really do want to tear down white society.

Thus far, it is apparent not only that more blacks at the low end of the income and education scale represent a greater threat than those at the high end in terms of saying they want to "tear down white society," but that the very people who expected them to want to do it are their counterparts, the least privileged in the non-Jewish white segment of New York society. The lines of polarization among the least privileged sectors of both societies are becoming apparent.

But the group which most shares the view that blacks want to tear down white society has yet to be looked at in detail. A breakdown of key groups within the Jewish community on the subject is presented in Table 40.

The results point clearly to the fact that among Jews the most apprehensive about blacks wanting to tear down white society were the Orthodox, those over 50, those with annual incomes under $10,000, and the least well educated.

Table 41 shows the opinion of the three main groups—Jews, blacks, and non-Jewish whites—as they divided by age and education. It is apparent that, true to the pattern observed in responses to other questions, the Jews showed themselves more apprehensive than non-Jewish whites on the issue of blacks' desire to tear down white society. This was true of younger and college-educated Jews as well as of older and less educated members of the group. However, within the Jewish community younger Jews and college-educated Jews were less apprehensive than older, less educated Jews. Within the non-Jewish white group, those with some college education believed less often than those with no college education that blacks want to tear down white society, and younger non-Jewish whites were more apt to say blacks do not want to tear down white society than were their elders.

Among blacks, those with a high school or college education denied they wanted to tear down white society more than those with only an eighth-grade education. All age groups strongly rejected such a goal, though those over 50 rejected it more strongly than those 49 and under.

It is fair to conclude that the least privileged Jews were more likely to believe that blacks want to upend white society, to tear it down. Thus, among non-Jewish whites, among the Jewish community, and among the blacks themselves, those relatively at the bottom end of the scale not only feared that blacks will tear down white society, but among blacks these are precisely the people who said they felt most prone to do it.

TABLE 40

BLACKS WANT TO TEAR DOWN WHITE SOCIETY: JEWISH OPINION

	Want %	Don't Want %	Not Sure %
Total Jewish	45	34	21
Orthodox	54	23	23
Conservative	46	30	24
Reform	50	32	18
Non-affiliated	30	51	19
21-34	39	43	18
35-49	46	36	18
50 and over	49	26	25
Under $10,000	52	23	25
$10,000-$15,000	40	42	18
Over $15,000	38	46	16
8th grade	58	14	28
High school	51	29	20
College	36	45	19

The converse is also the case, however. The best educated, most privileged members of all these groups tended to believe least that blacks want to break up and destroy white society. And, indeed, the more privileged blacks most denied such objectives themselves. It would appear that if the thrust for corrective action to avoid further polarization is to take place, it will have to be found by the better educated in all groups finding ways to communicate with and to persuade the less privileged members of their own segment of New York society. It should also be noted that younger Jews and non-Jewish whites were less apprehensive than their elders.

Tied to this reading of opinions on possible black motivations to tear down white society is the use of violence as a means for blacks to achieve their rights.

Before discussing the responses to questions on violence, it is interesting to look at some background material provided

TABLE 41

BLACKS WANT TO TEAR DOWN WHITE SOCIETY

	Want %	Don't Want %	Not Sure %
Total Jewish	45	34	21
21-34	39	43	18
35-49	46	36	18
50 and over	49	26	25
8th grade	58	14	28
High school	51	29	20
College	36	45	19
Total Blacks	20	69	11
21-34	22	66	12
35-49	22	66	12
50 and over	14	77	9
8th grade	31	54	15
High school	17	72	11
College	19	72	9
Total Non-Jewish White	31	44	25
21-34	30	48	22
35-49	33	38	29
50 and over	29	46	25
No college	32	40	28
Some college	25	57	18

by Gary Marx (see Table 42). In his study, for which the field work was conducted in 1964, blacks in certain urban areas were asked whether they agree or disagree with the statement "Violence will never help Negroes get equal rights." His sample was very much smaller than the one in the present study.

TABLE 42

VIOLENCE WILL NEVER HELP BLACKS GET EQUAL RIGHTS: NATIONAL URBAN, BLACKS, 1964

	Metro[a] %	N.Y. %	Chicago %	Atlanta %	Birmingham %
Agree	64	68	64	57	58
Disagree	29	27	32	39	35
Don't know	7	5	4	4	7

[a] Non-southern metropolitan area sample.
Source: Gary Marx, Protest and Prejudice (New York: Harper and Row, 1967), page 32.

The results from two national Louis Harris and Associates surveys of black attitudes, one conducted in the summer of 1963 and the other in the summer of 1966, also give the results of the study of New York opinion some sense of context (see Table 43).

The results of the study of the cross-section of New York City opinion on the question of blacks needing to use violence to win rights are shown in Table 44.

All groups in the city, including blacks, agreed in a rather lopsided fashion that blacks will not have to resort to violence to win their rights. But it is worth noting that white Catholics, Jews, and white Protestants were more convinced that violence can be avoided than were Puerto Ricans or blacks themselves.

The breakdown of the black group (Table 45) reveals significant differences; the pattern is sharp and clear. Obviously, the least convinced that blacks can win their objectives without resort to violence are the young and the best educated. The college-educated blacks yield less than a majority who expressed a belief that violence can be avoided. A rather high 37 percent of the 21-34 age group believed violence will be necessary.

The makings of tension between the Jewish and black communities become apparent. A plurality of Jews were convinced that blacks want to tear down white society. Among blacks, more of the younger and the college educated, though still a minority of both sections of the black community, expressed some doubt that blacks can indeed achieve their ends without the use of violence.

TABLE 43

BLACKS NEED TO USE VIOLENCE TO WIN RIGHTS: NATIONAL, BLACKS, 1963-1966

	1966 %	1963 %
Can win without violence	59	63
Will have to use violence	21	22
Not sure	20	15

TABLE 44

BLACKS NEED TO USE VIOLENCE TO WIN RIGHTS: CITY-WIDE

	Don't Need %	Must Use Violence %	Not Sure %
Total City	73	15	12
Jewish	78	12	10
Black	60	28	12
White Catholic	80	11	9
Puerto Rican	63	16	21
White Protestant	76	7	17

TABLE 45

BLACKS NEED TO USE VIOLENCE TO WIN RIGHTS: BLACKS

	Don't Need %	Must Use %	Not Sure %
Total Blacks	60	28	12
21-34	52	37	11
35-49	60	27	13
50+	73	14	13
8th grade	70	17	13
High school	59	29	12
College	49	39	12

Despite the relatively high percentage of Jews who said that blacks want to tear down white society, neither the Jewish nor any other group felt that the black militants are really representative of the views of most of the black community; this is true for the black community as well as other groups (see Table 46). However, once again, a higher proportion of blacks supported the black militants than the whites believed to be the case. This pattern once again shows itself to be centered among younger blacks (see Table 47).

Less than a majority of blacks under 35, albeit a plurality, said they don't go along with the black militants. To be sure, by a 48-34 percent margin they rejected the militants. But this is far below the 55-26 percent rejection for blacks as a group.

A mark of young people in all sectors of society in mid-1969 was a frustration with the way the establishment had run things. Clearly, the frustrations among young blacks are pushing them closer to the support of black militancy. It is significant, therefore, to recall that majorities of these same young blacks reject tearing down white society as a goal for blacks. However, if their nonviolent drive for equality is misinterpreted by dominant white society as a resort to violence and destruction of white society, then it is not beyond imagination to see the numbers supporting black militants rising rather than diminishing.

INTEGRATION OR SEPARATION?

Despite the disquieting sign just below the surface, the fact remains that at the time of this study a solid majority of all New York City still was committed to personally favoring integration of blacks into white society, rather than to a separate black society, as the figures in Table 48 show.

Once again, however, there were sharp differences, even though the largest group in each major ethnic segment favored integration. Least for integration were white Catholics, at 49 percent in support. Blacks themselves led, favoring it by 77-15 percent, followed by Puerto Ricans at 75-6 percent in support. White Protestants were not far behind these two groups, favoring integration by 68 to 19 percent. The Jewish division was 58 to 22 percent in support of integration. Yet within the Jewish group, there were some notable exceptions to the prevailing pattern of support for integration (see Table 49).

TABLE 46

REPRESENTATIVENESS OF BLACK MILITANTS' VIEWS: CITY-WIDE

	Do %	Do Not %	Not Sure %
Total City	13	67	20
Jewish	10	76	14
Black	26	55	19
White Catholic	9	73	18
Puerto Rican	15	51	34
White Protestant	8	71	21

TABLE 47

REPRESENTATIVENESS OF BLACK MILITANTS' VIEWS: BLACKS

	Total Blacks %	Age 21-34 %	Age 35-49 %	Age 50+ %
Black militants represent what I want	26	34	25	13
I don't go along with them	55	48	53	69
Not sure	19	18	22	18

TABLE 48

PERSONALLY WANT INTEGRATION OR SEPARATE BLACK SOCIETY: CITY-WIDE

	Integration %	Separate Society %	Not Sure %
Total City	64	19	17
Jewish	58	22	20
Black	77	15	8
White Catholic	49	29	22
Puerto Rican	75	6	18
White Protestant	68	19	13

HOW BLACKS ARE PERCEIVED

TABLE 49

PERSONALLY WANT INTEGRATION OR SEPARATE BLACK SOCIETY: JEWS

	Integration %	Separate Society %	Not Sure %
Total Jewish	58	22	20
Manhattan	69	13	18
Bronx	64	24	12
Queens	66	20	14
Brooklyn	43	29	28
Orthodox	40	37	23
Conservative	52	24	24
Reform	59	23	18
Non-affiliated	81	4	15
21-34	70	13	17
35-49	61	23	16
50 and over	47	29	24
8th grade	37	33	30
High school	49	29	22
College	72	13	15

Integration clearly carried the day except among Jewish residents in Brooklyn and those of Orthodox faith; in both groups, less than a majority supported it. A 55-year-old Brooklyn Jewish shopkeeper put it this way: "I think people are happier with their own kind. They are more at ease, more comfortable. I am with Jews. Let them be with their own Negroes. We can't mix anymore." A 26-year-old Orthodox Jew added: "It's what they want. It's best for them. This system of ours does not suit them." A 45-year-old lawyer in Brooklyn, earning $24,000 a year, said: "They've asked for it now, so why not give it to them. I am not prejudiced myself, but they have made an issue of separatism. Now let them see how they like living with it. We'll see how well they'll do then."

A majority of Jews did not share these views. A Jewish college graduate in the Bronx said: "Nobody in this world was

TABLE 50

FEELINGS BEHIND VIEWS ON
INTEGRATION/SEPARATION: JEWS

	Total Jewish %
Why Favor Integration	78
They are just as good as we are	18
Integration is natural	16
Would eliminate tensions	13
Less conflict in one society than two	9
Separatism is immoral	8
Blacks entitled to as good as whites	5
Blacks must be integrated	4
Necessary if equality is to be achieved	2
That's the way it is now	2
Would present no problems	1
Why Favor Separatism	24
They would rather live with own kind	12
Blacks and whites don't mix	4
Will take time before blacks ready for integration	3
They pull down the neighborhood	3
Blacks have no morals	1
They aren't human	1
Depends on Whether They Are Nice	8

made to be apart from anyone else. Everyone should live together." A Manhattan Jewish businessman added: "White society is doomed unless there is integration." A 27-year-old professional who lives in Queens said: "Integration is the right way. People must learn to share and live together. Segregation is all wrong." A 65-year-old Jewish Bronx woman who complained earlier that the "old neighborhood is going down with all these Puerto Ricans and Negroes moving in" nonetheless had this to say: "Everybody can find a place for himself in our society. This is a wealthy country. Why can't we all

HOW BLACKS ARE PERCEIVED

TABLE 51

PERSONALLY WANT INTEGRATION OR SEPARATE BLACK SOCIETY: NON-JEWISH WHITES

	Integration %	Separate Society %	Not Sure %
Total Jewish	58	22	20
21 - 34	70	13	17
35 - 49	61	23	16
50 and over	47	29	24
8th grade	37	33	30
High school	49	29	22
College	72	13	15
Total Non-Jewish White	61	20	19
21 - 34	69	17	14
35 - 49	61	18	21
50 and over	51	27	22
No college	58	21	21
some college	71	16	13

work and live together? Otherwise every minority, including the Jews, will be destroyed."

When all the volunteered comments among the Jewish group were added up, they emerged in statistical form as shown in Table 50.

Clearly, the dominant strain in Jewish thinking was that integration between the races is desirable because "they are just as good as we are," and also because it is "natural," "indefensible to oppose," and is the key to "eliminating tensions." But over one in five favored separatism.

Again, it is worth noting the age and education differences within the Jewish group and non-Jewish white group (see Table 51).

The young and the college-educated of both groups most strongly support integration, and those over 50 and those with less education showed less enthusiasm.

When the black community is analyzed in much the same detailed way, as shown in Table 52, it is immediately apparent that a sizable majority were committed to integration down the line.

The thrust for separatism is not high in any one sector, running at its peak among those under 35, those on welfare, and those earning below $3,000 a year and living in the Bronx. But scarcely more than one in five hold this view, even in these groups.

TABLE 52

PERSONALLY WANT INTEGRATION OR SEPARATE BLACK SOCIETY: BLACKS

	Integration %	Separate Society %	Not Sure %
Total Blacks	77	15	8
Manhattan	76	14	10
Bronx	76	20	4
Queens	80	11	9
Brooklyn	80	14	6
21-34	73	19	8
35-49	83	11	6
50+	80	11	9
8th grade	76	16	8
High school	78	15	7
College	78	14	8
Under $3,000	71	20	9
$3,000-$6,999	77	15	8
$7,000+	84	10	6
On welfare	71	21	8
Men	77	16	7
Women	79	13	8

TABLE 53

FEELINGS BEHIND VIEWS ON INTEGRATION/SEPARATION: BLACKS

	Total Blacks[a] %
Why Favor Integration:	
Only real way to equality	16
Dependent on each other, must live together	15
To learn to understand and work together	13
Together we build, divided we all fall	10
We are all human, all the same	8
Would cool things off, make for peace	6
Separation would tear down democracy	6
All are God's children, brothers	4
Will learn, progress faster	4
Only way a minority can get a voice	3
Why Favor Separation:	
Need to get on our own, without white man	9
They don't want us, we don't want them	3
More comfortable with own kind	2
Need black unity before can integrate	2
Not Sure	8

[a] Adds to more than 100 percent as some respondents volunteered more than one answer.

It is significant that the number of blacks on welfare, in the younger age category, and in the poverty group who believed in separatism is well below the number who felt that blacks must resort to violence.

The majority of blacks clearly disagree with separatism as a goal. A salesclerk in Manhattan, earning $6,000 a year, said: "We have spent three hundred years building this country up as slaves with our sweat and blood and we deserve to enjoy all the benefits. That means integration." A young black college student added: "Well, I've got my own thing now about black studies, but that's just a tactic. I won't be a whole man

TABLE 54

BLACKS IN NEW YORK CITY ARE JUSTIFIED IN DEMANDS: JEWS

	Are %	Are Not %	Depends[a] %	Not Sure %
Total Jewish	32	27	37	4
Manhattan	45	15	37	3
Bronx	38	30	30	2
Queens	31	25	39	5
Brooklyn	22	34	40	4
Orthodox	17	37	40	6
Conservative	26	34	36	4
Reform	25	28	41	6
Non-affiliated	60	8	31	1
21-34	45	19	34	2
35-49	33	22	42	3
50+	20	38	37	5
8th grade	15	33	45	7
High school	24	37	35	4
College	44	17	36	3

[a] Volunteered response.

until I'm accepted all the way in a completely integrated society where everyone is completely color blind."

The minority view among blacks was expressed by a 22-year-old unemployed black youth in the Jamaica section of Queens: "We should establish our own society to prove to ourselves that we can make it without the help of a white society. We are entitled to that opportunity." A black social worker in Brooklyn added: "We have been raised to dislike the Europeans. That's why our young will not accept integration anymore. We just won't get along."

A statistical summary of the volunteered comments by blacks on the subject of separatism versus integration is presented in Table 53.

HOW BLACKS ARE PERCEIVED

For all of the talk and recent action which would appear to signal a sharp black shift toward separatism, the fact remains that a substantial majority of blacks wanted integration, while a smaller percentage, though still a majority, of white society was willing to accept it.

ARE BLACK DEMANDS JUSTIFIED?

All of the nonblack groups in New York City were asked if they felt that blacks are justified or not in their demands. The pattern of responses among the Jewish group is shown in Table 54.

Again there were sharp variations among boroughs, Manhattan feeling most heavily that black demands are justified, followed by Jews in the Bronx and Queens not far behind. Brooklyn Jews trail far behind, as did Orthodox and Conservative Jews. In fact, Reform Jews also emerged slightly on the "not justified" side. That portion of the Jewish community which is not affiliated with the Jewish religion was decidedly on the side of the black demands. The younger Jews tended to feel by a wide margin that the blacks are justified, while those over 50 felt by almost two to one that they are not justified. The division by education is just as sharp, the college-educated Jews acknowledging black demands, while those with less than a high school education do not.

The Jewish cross-section was also asked if it felt the blacks were trying to get more than they are entitled to. The result: by 46 to 33 percent, most Jews felt blacks do not deserve what they want (see Table 55).

Once again, the answers show a sharply split Jewish community. In Manhattan and in Queens, there was less of a belief that blacks want to get more than they are entitled to than among Brooklyn and Bronx Jews. The Orthodox once more felt strongest that blacks are not entitled to what they are asking for, by a lopsided 58 to 18 percent. Older Jews shared this feeling, but younger Jews did not. The non-affiliated strongly disagreed with the statement by 58 to 24 percent. Those earning under $10,000 felt blacks are unrealistic in their demands, while those earning over $10,000 annually were more evenly divided. Finally, the Jews with only an eighth-grade education felt blacks are asking for more than they are entitled to by 59 to 8 percent, while the college educated deny the proposition by 44 to 38 percent.

TABLE 55

BLACKS WANT MORE THAN THEY ARE ENTITLED TO: JEWS

	Do %	Don't %	Not Sure %
Total Jewish	46	33	21
Manhattan	35	40	25
Bronx	53	35	12
Queens	42	42	16
Brooklyn	52	21	27
Orthodox	58	18	24
Conservative	53	25	22
Reform	49	31	20
Non-affiliated	24	58	18
21-34	37	44	19
35-49	43	35	22
50+	55	23	22
Under $10,000	51	24	25
$10,000-$15,000	42	43	15
Over $15,000	40	37	23
8th grade	59	8	33
High school	51	29	20
College	38	44	18

The pattern among non-Jewish whites parallels the Jewish divisions by age (see Table 56).

The young and the college educated tended to believe black demands are justified, while the older and no-college groups did not. Italians tended to feel more strongly than the Irish that black demands are not justified. The full tide of opposition to black demands can be observed most clearly in the special "backlash" sample of non-Jewish whites, those who live in areas which voted 80 percent or more against the Civilian Review Board. A sizable and clear plurality of each group opposed black demands. But the Catholics tended to be more in

TABLE 56

BLACKS IN NEW YORK CITY ARE JUSTIFIED IN DEMANDS: NON-JEWISH WHITES

	Are %	Are Not %	Depends[a] %	Not Sure %
Total Non-Jewish Whites	36	23	35	6
21-34	43	19	33	5
35-49	34	23	34	9
50 and over	27	28	38	7
No college	32	23	37	8
Some college	47	22	28	3
Italian	26	38	29	7
Irish	18	29	51	2

[a] Volunteered response.

opposition than the non-Catholics, those over 50 more opposed than those under 35, those with no college education more opposed than those with some college education.

Once again, the patterns of difference among all groups by age, borough, and education emerge clearly. Those in New York City in solid opposition to black demands were older and less affluent Jews, particularly those in Brooklyn. Among non-Jewish whites, opposition was heaviest among white Catholics, especially those who are older and less affluent. By the same token, there were pockets of support for black demands among the young and the affluent, almost irrespective of ethnic background. Indeed, not only are there attitudinal differences in New York City between blacks and whites, but also between the old and the young, the affluent and the non-affluent.

TABLE 57

BLACKS IN NEW YORK CITY ARE JUSTIFIED
IN DEMANDS: "BACKLASH" WHITES

	Are %	Are Not %	Depends[a] %	Not Sure %
Total				
"Backlash" Whites	15	42	39	4
Catholic	12	43	39	6
Non-Catholic	23	38	35	4
Italian	15	40	41	4
Irish	15	46	35	4
21-34	16	34	47	3
35-49	18	39	38	5
50 and over	11	54	29	6
No college	14	43	38	5
Some college	19	36	42	3

[a] Volunteered response.

PACE OF BLACKS IN NEW YORK CITY

Far less than a majority of whites were convinced of the justice of black demands, and blacks in New York City also found themselves as far apart from the rest of the community on the question of whether or not they are moving too fast, too slow, or at about the right pace.

City-wide, almost three times as many people thought blacks have been going at too fast rather than too slow a pace, although it should be pointed out that the number who said "too slow" or "about right" approximates the "too fast" group. The splits by key divisions within New York are dramatic and sharp. Seventy-six percent of the special "backlash" sample from areas overwhelmingly against the Civilian Review Board were convinced blacks are going too fast, and a majority of both the Jewish (59 percent) and the white Catholic (55 percent) groups also said "too fast."

HOW BLACKS ARE PERCEIVED 65

TABLE 58

PACE OF BLACKS IN NEW YORK CITY: CITY-WIDE

	Too Fast %	Too Slow %	About Right %	Not Sure %
Total City	44	16	27	13
Jewish	59	8	17	16
Black	15	45	32	8
White Catholic	55	8	25	12
Puerto Rican	38	10	36	16
White Protestant	48	10	29	13
"Backlash" non-Jewish white	76	1	13	10
White union	59	8	21	12
Black union	15	46	33	6
Jewish men	58	9	19	14
Jewish women	59	9	15	17
Manhattan	32	17	37	14
Bronx	37	14	34	15
Queens	65	6	19	10
Brooklyn	61	6	19	14
Richmond	60	6	26	8

By contrast, less than a majority of white Protestants (48 percent) felt this way, and a much lower number of Puerto Ricans (38 percent) shared the same feeling. However, it is significant that only the black groups--the black group as a whole as well as black union members--emerged with the largest proportions in the "too slow" category. Bronx and Manhattan opinion differed sharply from that in Queens, Brooklyn, and Richmond.

Certainly there is a substantial amount of feeling among whites in New York that the pace of black demands should be at least leveled out, and certainly not increased.

Valuable for the sake of comparison are the answers whites gave to the question of pace of blacks in national Harris surveys conducted in the summers of 1963 and 1966 (see Table 59).

TABLE 59

PACE OF BLACKS: NATIONAL, WHITES, 1963-1966

	Total 1966 %	Total 1963 %
Too fast	70	64
Too slow	4	6
About right	14	17
Not sure	12	13

The results show that fewer New Yorkers said "too fast" in 1969 (Table 58) than white Americans in 1963 or 1966. However, this still does not alter the fact that in New York in mid-1969 a substantial number of whites thought the pace of blacks was too fast.

Whether the admonition from New York's white community will be heeded by blacks is not entirely certain, as a breakdown of blacks on the same question clearly shows (see Table 60).

The fact that 52 percent of the under-35 group, 50 percent of the 8th-grade-educated, and a significant 54 percent of the black college-educated group all said "too slow" points to a substantial feeling of dissatisfaction in New York's black community. There is no doubt where those dissatisfied are in the black community: among the poorest, the well educated, and especially the young.

The division in the Jewish community reveals the familiar lines of disagreement: the young, Manhattan residents, and the college educated are on one side, and the older, less affluent, grade school or high school educated, and Brooklyn Jews are on the other side (Table 61).

The reason most frequently cited by Jews (20 percent) as to why they thought blacks are moving too fast was "too much violence, rioting." Many compared the way blacks are trying to achieve equality with their personal view of how the Jews made it. A 67-year-old Jewish skilled craftsman in Brooklyn illustrated this point of view when he said: "They want everything on a silver platter. We Jews also had to fight for jobs and houses, but we didn't use guns." A 26-year-old Jewish salesman in Brooklyn, earning $13,000 a year, said: "The

TABLE 60

PACE OF BLACKS IN NEW YORK CITY: BLACKS

	Too Fast %	Too Slow %	About Right %	Not Sure %
Total Blacks	15	45	32	8
21-34	9	52	31	8
35-39	15	45	33	7
50+	25	33	35	7
8th grade	15	50	27	8
High school	16	41	35	8
College	12	54	26	8

TABLE 61

PACE OF BLACKS IN NEW YORK CITY: JEWS

	Too Fast %	Too Slow %	About Right %	Not Sure %
Total Jewish	59	8	17	16
Manhattan	35	17	28	20
Bronx	56	5	23	16
Queens	66	9	15	10
Brooklyn	69	5	10	16
Orthodox	71	1	14	14
Conservative	70	1	15	14
Reform	64	6	14	16
Non-affiliated	31	24	25	20
21-34	47	16	21	16
35-49	56	10	18	16
50+	71	2	13	14
8th grade	71	-	12	17
High school	71	2	15	12
College	46	17	21	16

TABLE 62

FEELINGS BEHIND VIEWS ON PACE OF BLACKS: JEWS

	Total Jewish %
Why Too Fast	67
Too much violence, rioting	20
Want things they don't deserve	12
Trying to make up for lost time	12
Want to dominate everything	7
Want things not ready for	6
Too much tension in education	4
Should do it more rationally	3
Confused among themselves	2
Taking past hurts out on us	1
Why Too Slow	8
Waited too long for gradualism	4
Entitled to much more	3
Still much discrimination	1
Why About Right	15
Have to push to get anywhere	9
Finally making gains	4
Right direction, wrong methods	1
Those with ability get ahead	1
Not Sure	10

Negro is using violence as his secret weapon, and I'll never give in to that." A 46-year-old Jewish foreman in Brooklyn earning $8,000 explained his feelings this way: "They claim they were sold into slavery. It was their own people who sold them. They want too much too fast. We Jews had to work a long time to get it." A 42-year-old Jewish social worker in Manhattan was indignant: "They just want to walk in and take over everything--the schools, business, colleges. Let them work and sweat for it in an orderly manner, not just grab and run. Who do they think they are anyway?" A young Jewish

HOW BLACKS ARE PERCEIVED

accountant in Brooklyn put it this way: "They're now trying to get into the colleges and the professional jobs by just saying we're Negro and deserve it. Well, they have to do it by studying, taking competitive exams, and doing their damnedest in high school and the city colleges just the way we Jews have always done it. We'd feel cheated if they got it without work, when we've always worked so hard for it."

When all of the Jewish comments are added up, the statistical results of their feelings are as shown in Table 62.

Though among the city's ethnic groups the Jews showed the greatest degree of concern over crime and racial tension, they felt little threat from the blacks to their own status or jobs. Rather, some Jews expressed a deep-felt resentment that they had worked so hard and for so long that they are bitter at the thought of the blacks making it any more easily than they did.

The pattern among non-Jewish whites shows that older people were more concerned about blacks going too fast than were young people; that Catholics were more concerned than non-Catholics; and that those who had not been to college were much more concerned than those who had been to college (see Table 63).

TABLE 63

PACE OF BLACKS IN NEW YORK CITY: NON-JEWISH WHITES

	Too Fast %	Too Slow %	About Right %	Not Sure %
Total Non-Jewish Whites	48	10	29	13
21-34	44	14	26	16
35-49	48	8	32	12
50+	55	6	27	12
Catholic	50	8	29	13
Non-Catholic	42	15	28	15
Italian	62	7	22	9
Irish	59	7	22	12
No college	50	8	27	15
Some college	37	16	35	12

Though the reasons cited by non-Jewish whites were similar to those given by the Jews, the tone of comment was somewhat different. Illustrative was a 26-year-old Catholic in Brooklyn: "If they keep us these threats of violence, they are going to catch it, but good. We got a little muscle, too, you know." A 21-year-old assistant store manager in Queens put it this way: "They're just plain lazy and not working. They're all on welfare on my money. Only one in ten of them will work." In Brooklyn, a 37-year-old housewife said: "All of a sudden after all these years they want everything for nothing all at once. They are getting more than the whites and whites have to work for it, they don't." A 49-year-old Catholic housewife in Queens added: "They keep saying they were slaves and what was denied them 100 years ago. I didn't deny them anything. Let them go to work for a change."

The recurrent theme of "let them stop asking for something for nothing" also runs through the non-Jewish white group. But there was less of a tendency on the part of non-Jewish whites to make comparisons between themselves and the blacks

TABLE 64

PACE OF BLACKS IN NEW YORK CITY

	Too Fast %	Too Slow %	About Right %	Not Sure %
Total Jewish	59	8	17	16
21-34	47	16	21	16
35-49	56	10	18	16
50 and over	71	2	13	14
8th grade	71	-	12	17
High school	71	2	15	12
College	46	17	21	16
Total Non-Jewish Whites	48	10	29	13
21-34	44	14	26	16
35-49	48	8	32	12
50 and over	55	6	27	12
No college	50	8	27	15
Some college	37	16	35	12

than there was among the Jews. Non-Jewish whites were more apt to assert that blacks "really have little character or desire to earn what they want to achieve."

Differences within both the Jewish and non-Jewish white communities should be noted. Examining the age and education breakdowns of both groups in New York City (Table 64), it is apparent that younger and college-educated Jews showed themselves to be substantially less worried by the pace of black demands than older and less educated Jews. In the non-Jewish white group there is a similar division, the college educated saying "too fast" less often than the non-college-educated, and the young saying it less often than their elders.

DISCRIMINATION AGAINST BLACKS

The pace of black demands clearly bothered the white majority. But part of the reason for the sharply differing estimates of the situation by blacks and Jews and by blacks and white Catholics stems from quite a different set of conditions. Blacks and whites have very different perceptions of whether or not blacks are discriminated against in specific situations. Responses to a series of questions specifying kinds of discrimination are shown in Table 65.

Out of Twelve specific areas of possible discrimination tested, in only two did majorities of adults in New York City feel that blacks are discriminated against: in renting apartments in mixed or white neighborhoods and in getting decent housing. The pattern among Jews shows that fewer of this group believed blacks are discriminated against than the average for the city. In no case did a majority of white Catholics feel blacks are the victims of discrimination and in only one of the twelve areas did even a plurality feel that it exists for blacks. White Protestants, who consistently were the most sympathetic group toward blacks outside of the Puerto Rican and black communities, saw discrimination by at least a plurality in five out of the twelve cases.

By contrast, blacks saw discrimination against themselves by an overwhelming majority in eleven of the twelve situations and by a sizable plurality in the remaining situation.

When it comes down to specific discrimination in housing, employment, getting into labor unions, the prices paid in grocery stores, education, and the way they are treated by the police, blacks felt deeply that they are given second-class

TABLE 65

PERCEPTION OF SPECIFIC DISCRIMINATION AGAINST BLACKS: CITY-WIDE

	Total City %	Jewish %	Black %	White Catholic %	Puerto Rican %	White Protestant %
Renting Apartments in Mixed or White Neighborhoods						
Discriminated against	60	55	82	46	56	63
Not discriminated against	27	33	11	38	24	25
Not sure	13	12	7	16	20	12
Getting Decent Housing						
Discriminated against	59	55	87	41	60	58
Not discriminated against	29	34	9	46	22	31
Not sure	12	11	4	13	18	11
Getting Skilled Labor Jobs						
Discriminated against	48	40	82	29	42	60
Not discriminated against	37	44	11	59	27	33
Not sure	15	16	7	12	31	7
Getting White Collar Office Jobs						
Discriminated against	46	40	79	27	43	46
Not discriminated against	40	45	15	59	31	43
Not sure	14	15	6	14	26	11
Rent They Pay						
Discriminated against	43	37	79	20	51	35
Not discriminated against	37	39	13	57	29	42
Not sure	20	24	8	23	20	23
Getting into Labor Unions						
Discriminated against	40	33	74	21	38	40
Not discriminated against	34	34	13	53	27	37
Not sure	26	33	13	26	35	23

	Total City %	Jewish %	Black %	White Catholic %	Puerto Rican %	White Protestant %
Grocery Prices They Pay						
Discriminated against	38	29	79	21	42	30
Not discriminated against	41	51	12	55	31	48
Not sure	21	20	9	24	27	22
Wages They Are Paid						
Discriminated against	39	33	78	16	48	29
Not discriminated against	45	50	13	65	31	56
Not sure	16	17	9	19	21	15
Getting Quality Education in Public Schools						
Discriminated against	37	25	76	22	35	33
Not discriminated against	50	66	16	69	38	45
Not sure	13	9	8	9	27	22
Way Treated by Police						
Discriminated against	33	24	66	15	43	28
Not discriminated against	49	60	17	71	30	57
Not sure	18	16	17	14	27	15
Getting Manual Labor Jobs						
Discriminated against	26	17	49	15	32	24
Not discriminated against	61	72	42	74	45	64
Not sure	13	11	9	11	23	12
Way Their Kids Treated by White Teachers						
Discriminated against	23	13	60	8	27	18
Not discriminated against	54	72	18	73	39	49
Not sure	23	15	22	19	34	33

treatment. In New York City, in mid-1969, except for the Puerto Ricans, the blacks were virtually alone in this feeling.

There is probably no other finding of this study which points up more strikingly the gap in communication and understanding between the blacks and the Jewish and white Catholic communities. It is almost as though both the blacks and whites were living in different worlds, instead of the same city.

In the area of housing, three situations were described.

In getting apartments in mixed or white areas, a majority of 82 percent of the blacks felt discriminated against, whereas only 55 percent of the Jews, 46 percent of the white Catholics, 56 percent of the Puerto Ricans, and 63 percent of the white Protestants felt blacks were the victims of discrimination in this situation.

In getting decent housing, 87 percent of blacks felt discriminated against; 55 percent of the Jews, 41 percent of the white Catholics, 60 percent of the Puerto Ricans, and 58 percent of the white Protestants agreed with this perception.

In the rent they pay, a high 79 percent of the blacks felt discriminated against; 51 percent of the Puerto Ricans agreed, but only 37 percent of the Jews, 20 percent of the white Catholics, and 35 percent of the white Protestants shared the blacks' view.

In the area of employment; five situations were described.

In getting skilled labor jobs, 82 percent of the blacks felt discriminated against, a view shared in the majority only by 60 percent of white Protestants. But only 40 percent of the Jews, 42 percent of the Puerto Ricans, and 29 percent of the white Catholics agreed.

In getting white collar office jobs, 79 percent of blacks felt discriminated against. Forty percent of the Jews, 27 percent of the white Catholics, 43 percent of the Puerto Ricans, and 46 percent of the white Protestants said they believed such discrimination exists.

In getting into labor unions, a sizable 74 percent of the blacks felt they are victims of discrimination, while only 33 percent of the Jewish group, 21 percent of the white Catholics, 38 percent of the Puerto Ricans, and 40 percent of the white Protestants felt that this kind of discrimination against blacks exists.

In the wages they are paid, 78 percent of the blacks felt discriminated against, but only 48 percent of the Puerto Ricans, 33 percent of the Jews, 29 percent of the white Protestants, and 16 percent of the white Catholics agreed.

HOW BLACKS ARE PERCEIVED

In getting manual labor jobs, 49 percent of the blacks felt discriminated against, whereas 32 percent of the Puerto Ricans, 24 percent of the white Protestants, 17 percent of the Jews, and 15 percent of the white Catholics held that blacks are discriminated against in this way.

In the area of education, two situations were described.

In getting a quality education for their children in the public schools, 76 percent of the blacks felt they suffer from discrimination, but only 35 percent of the Puerto Ricans, 33 percent of the white Protestants, 25 percent of the Jews, and 22 percent of the white Catholics perceived the black situation this way.

In the way their children are treated by white teachers, 60 percent of the blacks felt discriminated against, but only 27 percent of the Puerto Ricans, 18 percent of the WASPs, 13 percent of the Jews, and 8 percent of the white Catholics shared this view.

Two additional situations were described. In the prices they pay in their grocery stores, 79 percent of the blacks felt discriminated against, whereas 42 percent of Puerto Ricans, 30 percent of white Protestants, 29 percent of the Jews, and 21 percent of the white Catholic group believed it to be so. In the way they are treated by the police, 66 percent of the blacks felt they are discriminated against, but only 43 percent of the Puerto Ricans, 28 percent of the WASPs, 24 percent of the Jews, and 15 percent of the white Catholics felt the same way.

With only minor exceptions, blacks are isolated in their view of discrimination against them. In addition, the order of those sympathetic to the blacks' plight is fairly consistent. Puerto Ricans tended to empathize most with the claim of discrimination, white Protestants came next, Jews next to last, and white Catholics last. The Catholics perceived significantly less discrimination against blacks in all twelve cases than did the other groups.

There are some important differences discernible within both the Jewish and non-Jewish white communities on alleged discrimination against blacks. The division in the Jewish community is summarized in Table 66.

Among Manhattan Jews, at least a plurality believed that blacks are discriminated against in ten out of the twelve specific situations. In Queens, Jews saw blacks discriminated against in four out of the twelve specific situations. In the Bronx, Jews believed blacks are discriminated against in two out of twelve areas. In Brooklyn, in none of the situations did even a plurality believe there is discrimination against blacks.

TABLE 66

PERCEPTION OF SPECIFIC DISCRIMINATION AGAINST BLACKS IN CITY: JEWS

	Total Jewish %	Man. %	Brx %	Quns %	Bklyn %	Orth %	Cons %	Ref %	Non-Affil %	21-34 %	35-49 %	50+ %	8th Gr %	HS %	Col %
Renting Apartments in Mixed or White Neighborhoods															
Discriminated against	55	69	52	66	41	45	47	55	73	66	58	45	34	48	67
Not discriminated against	33	22	40	22	44	39	41	33	19	26	32	40	49	38	24
Not sure	12	9	8	12	15	16	12	12	8	8	10	15	17	14	9
Getting Decent Housing															
Discriminated against	55	72	51	63	41	40	45	56	69	68	61	39	31	47	69
Not discriminated against	34	15	44	29	42	43	44	32	17	24	26	46	55	40	22
Not sure	11	13	5	8	17	17	11	12	14	8	13	15	14	13	9
Getting Skilled Jobs															
Discriminated against	40	63	41	44	25	27	29	41	63	56	40	27	18	30	55
Not discriminated against	44	27	44	37	60	53	54	45	24	30	48	54	62	53	32
Not sure	16	10	15	19	15	20	17	14	13	14	12	19	20	17	13
Getting White Collar Office Jobs															
Discriminated against	40	55	40	42	30	28	31	40	61	53	45	25	24	32	51
Not discriminated against	45	27	49	43	54	51	54	46	29	33	39	58	58	53	35
Not sure	15	18	11	15	16	21	15	14	10	14	16	17	18	15	14
Rent They Pay															
Discriminated against	37	58	34	39	25	25	27	36	60	49	42	23	16	30	49
Not discriminated against	39	17	54	42	40	45	50	39	22	30	36	49	62	44	28
Not sure	24	25	12	19	35	30	23	25	18	21	22	28	22	26	23
Wages They Are Paid															
Discriminated against	33	54	24	40	22	20	23	34	55	47	40	18	12	27	
Not discriminated against	50	27	66	46	59	62	60	52	26	38	47	63	73	58	38
Not sure	17	19	10	14	19	18	17	14	19	15	13	19	15	15	17

76

	Total Jewish %	Man. %	Brx %	Quns %	Bklyn %	Orth %	Cons %	Ref %	Non-Affil %	21-34 %	35-49 %	50+ %	8th Gr %	HS %	Col %
Getting into Labor Unions															
Discriminated against	33	48	32	37	23	22	24	33	53	45	36	22	15	27	44
Not discriminated against	34	32	42	25	38	39	41	36	20	25	32	44	54	38	26
Not sure	33	20	16	38	39	39	35	31	27	30	32	34	31	35	30
Grocery Prices They Pay															
Discriminated against	29	52	20	37	14	13	18	28	57	39	36	14	6	20	43
Not discriminated against	51	28	70	46	57	65	61	50	28	38	46	66	73	58	39
Not sure	20	20	10	17	29	22	21	22	15	23	18	20	21	22	18
Getting Quality Education for Their Kids															
Discriminated against	25	49	23	28	11	7	12	23	58	41	27	11	5	18	38
Not discriminated against	66	39	67	65	82	83	79	70	32	54	62	79	91	73	54
Not sure	9	12	10	7	7	10	9	7	10	5	11	10	4	9	8
Way Treated by Police															
Discriminated against	24	48	17	29	10	13	10	23	50	39	25	10	--	18	35
Not discriminated against	60	27	70	37	75	69	74	61	36	46	58	73	80	68	47
Not sure	16	25	13	34	15	18	16	16	14	15	17	17	20	14	18
Getting Manual Labor Jobs															
Discriminated against	17	34	14	16	9	10	9	16	33	25	20	8	4	14	23
Not discriminated against	72	51	75	71	81	80	81	74	53	64	67	80	88	75	64
Not sure	11	15	11	13	10	10	10	10	14	11	13	12	8	11	13
Way Their Kids Treated by White Teachers															
Discriminated against	13	28	9	16	4	2	4	11	35	23	15	3	--	8	21
Not discriminated against	72	46	78	68	85	83	86	76	43	60	73	81	91	78	60
Not sure	15	26	13	16	11	15	10	13	22	17	12	16	9	14	19

TABLE 67

PERCEPTION OF SPECIFIC DISCRIMINATION AGAINST BLACKS IN CITY:
NON-JEWISH WHITES

	Total Non-Jewish Whites %	21-34 %	35-49 %	50+ %	Cath %	Non-Cath %	Ital %	Irish %	No Col %	Some Col %	Union Memb %
Renting Apt. in Mixed or White Neighborhoods											
Discriminated against	54	62	50	46	50	67	45	63	50	65	51
Not discriminated against	30	24	28	40	32	22	41	20	32	22	34
Not sure	16	14	22	14	18	11	14	17	18	13	15
Getting Decent Housing											
Discriminated against	51	65	45	39	47	63	38	50	45	71	47
Not discriminated against	34	25	35	46	36	26	51	37	38	22	43
Not sure	15	10	20	15	17	11	11	13	17	7	10
Getting Skilled Jobs											
Discriminated against	40	48	34	34	33	59	26	37	32	63	36
Not discriminated against	42	37	40	55	46	32	63	46	47	29	48
Not sure	18	15	26	11	21	9	11	17	21	8	16
Getting White Collar Office Jobs											
Discriminated against	36	46	30	30	32	48	27	43	31	53	34
Not discriminated against	46	41	46	55	48	42	63	46	49	37	52
Not sure	18	13	24	15	20	10	10	11	20	10	14
Getting into Unions											
Discriminated against	31	36	31	22	26	44	22	28	25	48	26
Not discriminated against	41	36	37	53	43	34	58	52	46	25	51
Not sure	28	28	32	25	31	22	20	20	29	27	23
Getting Quality Education in Public Schools											
Discriminated against	29	39	23	21	25	38	19	22	23	44	28
Not discriminated against	55	50	53	64	59	44	75	61	58	44	59
Not sure	16	11	14	15	16	18	6	17	19	12	13

	Total Non-Jewish Whites %	21-34 %	35-49 %	50+ %	Cath %	Non-Cath %	Ital %	Irish %	No Col %	Some Col %	Union Memb %
Grocery Prices They Pay											
Discriminated against	28	41	28	10	27	33	19	17	24	43	28
Not discriminated against	46	39	46	60	47	46	64	48	50	35	53
Not sure	26	20	26	30	26	21	17	35	26	22	19
Wages They Are Paid											
Discriminated against	27	38	26	12	25	33	16	11	25	35	28
Not discriminated against	53	46	50	67	53	50	70	67	54	48	59
Not sure	20	16	24	21	22	17	14	22	21	17	13
Way Treated by Police											
Discriminated against	25	37	23	10	24	29	12	13	21	38	25
Not discriminated against	55	48	52	71	56	53	76	78	58	46	61
Not sure	20	15	25	19	20	18	12	9	21	16	14
Getting Manual Jobs											
Discriminated against	22	29	19	15	20	28	16	11	19	29	25
Not discriminated against	62	56	61	72	63	59	77	70	64	55	65
Not sure	16	15	20	13	17	13	7	19	27	16	10
Way Kids Treated by White Teachers											
Discriminated against	15	22	15	5	13	22	5	4	13	22	15
Not discriminated against	58	53	58	65	61	48	79	74	60	53	66
Not sure	27	25	27	30	26	30	16	22	27	25	19
Rent They Pay											
Discriminated against	31	41	31	18	29	39	19	17	28	42	31
Not discriminated against	44	40	42	54	46	37	63	54	47	34	49
Not sure	25	19	27	28	25	24	18	29	25	24	20

Similarly, Orthodox Jews found discrimination against blacks less than either Conservative or Reform Jews, while non-affiliated Jews believed by strong majorities in ten out of the twelve situations that discrimination exists.

In an age division, the differences are dramatic. Among Jews under 35, blacks were believed to be discriminated against in eight of the twelve cases. But Jews over 50 could see discrimination in only one of the twelve, and only a plurality believed there is discrimination in that one area. The education pattern parallels the age cut: Jews with some college education perceived discrimination against blacks in eight of the twelve situations, while those who never went to high school did not believe it exists in any of the twelve cases.

Clearly, among the Jews in New York City there are two major camps--with the young, the educated, the non-affiliated, and those who live in Manhattan in one, and the older, the less well educated, the Orthodox, and residents of Brooklyn in the other. The differences are of such a magnitude that in the area of racial discrimination it is impossible to make generalizations about a cohesive Jewish group. One part of the Jewish community in New York clearly showed an awareness of discrimination against blacks. And this awareness suggests they are ready to go a long way toward making accommodations with blacks, for they have become convinced real injustices exist. But a larger group did not see it this way at all. They did not recognize that discrimination exists.

When the entire non-Jewish, non-black remainder of New York's adult population is analyzed in detail, similar differences emerge (see Table 67).

On an over-all basis, the non-Jewish, non-black population of New York said it believes discrimination against blacks exists in only two out of the twelve situations. By age, the under-35 group perceived discrimination in six out of the twelve cases, but the over-50 group perceived discrimination one of the twelve situations. Catholics (including Puerto Ricans in this case) believed that discrimination exists in only two of the twelve situations, but among non-Catholics it was seen in six of the twelve situations. Among Italians no discrimination was believed to exist in eleven of the twelve situations, and the Irish saw no discrimination in ten of the twelve. Those with no college education perceived discrimination in only two of the twelve situations, but the college educated saw it in seven of the twelve situations.

TABLE 68

PERCEPTION OF POLICE TREATMENT OF BLACKS IN CITY: CITY-WIDE

	Use Brutality %	Too Lenient %	Fair %	Not Sure %
Total City	25	17	38	20
Jewish	18	23	42	17
Black	48	8	24	20
White Catholic	13	26	47	14
Puerto Rican	37	8	26	29
White Protestant	25	15	36	24
Manhattan	40	9	23	28
Bronx	27	13	45	15
Queens	17	21	46	16
Brooklyn	18	23	40	19
Richmond	12	31	44	13

TABLE 69

PERCEPTION OF POLICE TREATMENT OF BLACKS IN CITY: BLACKS

	Use Brutality %	Too Lenient %	Fair %	Not Sure %
Total Blacks	48	8	24	20
Manhattan	44	14	20	22
Bronx	51	5	23	21
Queens	59	4	17	20
Brooklyn	46	5	31	18
21-34	58	6	40	16
35-49	45	7	24	24
50+	33	14	34	19
8th grade	38	11	29	22
High school	49	7	24	20
College	56	6	21	17

POLICE TREATMENT OF BLACKS

One of the widest differences between the black community and the rest of New York exists in the estimate of how the city police treat the blacks. The entire sample was asked if the police use brutality on blacks, are too lenient, or are fair to blacks.

The results, shown in Table 68, are more mixed than in the case of direct discrimination. Blacks clearly tended to believe that police brutality exists against them. But Puerto Ricans were not far behind in making a similar assessment, and white Protestants tended to agree with them. However, though a plurality of both Jewish and white Catholic opinion said the police are fair to blacks, twice as many of these groups as blacks thought the police to be too lenient with blacks.

Again, however, within the black community, there are definite and distinct segments which obviously are aroused on the police brutality issue.

Blacks in Queens and the Bronx, those under 35, and the better educated all claimed police brutality in majority numbers. Many of the blacks said they have experienced brutality themselves or have seen it "with my own eyes." An unemployed 24-year-old Negro from the South Bronx put it this way: "I've seen it all right. They treat you like dogs." A 55-year-old skilled craftsman in Queens, who earns over $14,000, said: "Sure the police do that. I've seen with these old eyes the police manhandling men, women, and children while placing them under arrest." In the Bronx, a 28-year-old black foreman reported: "The other night I saw a group of kids sitting on a stoop and the police came along and started swinging their clubs for no reason at all." A 62-year-old man on welfare in Harlem added: "I see so much of it, just about every day. The police beat the blacks first and then ask them to explain later."

Not all blacks shared these views. A number said that some police violence is inevitable and "some cops are good and some are bad." A 38-year-old black in Manhattan commented: "The police have a duty to perform. Too many people are looking for trouble and resist the police at every turn, even if they are hurt." A 22-year-old black clerk added: "With some blacks who are bad, you would have to use police brutality to keep them in line." A 37-year-old unskilled laborer in Harlem said: "If you ask me, the police ought to bang a few more heads, especially among the young ones."

TABLE 70

FEELINGS BEHIND FEELINGS ABOUT POLICE TREATMENT OF BLACKS: BLACKS

	Total Blacks[a] %
Engage in Brutality:	52
Had experience, seen it myself	13
Unnecessarily shove and beat people	9
Heard of it, read complaints about it	9
Police are personally racists	9
They are white, and whites dislike blacks	7
Police don't try to understand blacks	3
If they need an arrest, they arrest a black	1
Brutality obvious in poor neighborhoods	1
Are Fair:	30
Law and order necessary, people bound to get hurt	8
Black cops bad too sometimes, cops good and bad	7
Never seen them unfair	6
Police try to treat people equally	5
Police have to take a lot, sometimes rough	4
Too Lenient:	6
Trouble, and failure of law and order proves it	4
They are indifferent, stand around, do nothing	2
Not Sure	15

[a] Adds to more than 100 percent as some respondents volunteered more than one answer.

A summary of the volunteered views of blacks on police brutality is shown in Table 70.

The police brutality question has many different dimensions, including confidence in the police generally, quite apart from its special racial overtones. Some of these implications can be seen in a breakdown of the white Catholic group, shown in Table 71.

TABLE 71

PERCEPTION OF POLICE TREATMENT OF BLACKS IN CITY: WHITE CATHOLICS

	Use Brutality %	Too Lenient %	Fair %	Not Sure %
Total White Catholic	13	26	47	14
Italian	11	24	52	13
Irish	9	33	48	10
White Catholic "Backlash" non-Jewish	6	29	54	11

It is evident that the Italian group, which consistently on straightout black-white issues showed the least empathy for blacks, were less convinced that police are too lenient with blacks than were the Irish. In fact, the Irish group appeared to feel the police are too lenient more than did any other group, at least among white Catholics, undoubtedly indicating strong attachments among them for the police. They even felt more strongly on this score than the special oversample which voted over 80 percent against a Civilian Review Board.

A breakdown among the Jewish group on the same question again reveals sharp splits within the Jewish community. The difference between Manhattan and Brooklyn Jews is both dramatic and real, as is the difference between non-affiliated Jews and both Orthodox and Conservative Jews. Brooklyn Jews, joined by their Orthodox and Conservative brethren, tended to believe that the police mollycoddle the blacks in the city. So do Jews over 50 years of age. But more than any group in the entire city, Jewish people with only an eighth-grade education felt most strongly that the police have been too lenient with blacks (see Table 73).

Comparing the age and education cuts in the black community (Table 69), the Jewish community (Table 72), and the non-Jewish white community (Table 73), both younger Jews and younger nonwhites were more apt to say that there was brutality than were older persons, and the college educated in both these groups were also more apt to say there was brutality. The breakdown is similar among blacks, though in that group the young and the college educated take that position by substantial majorities.

HOW BLACKS ARE PERCEIVED

TABLE 72

PERCEPTION OF POLICE TREATMENT OF BLACKS IN CITY: JEWS

	Use Brutality %	Too Lenient %	Fair %	Not Sure %
Total Jewish	18	23	42	17
Manhattan	46	13	15	26
Bronx	13	19	55	13
Queens	15	18	51	16
Brooklyn	7	34	43	16
Orthodox	5	30	52	13
Conservative	8	30	47	15
Reform	14	24	47	15
Non-affiliated	45	8	22	25
21-34	28	20	34	18
35-49	24	20	34	22
50 and over	5	27	53	15
8th grade	--	38	46	16
High school	11	27	49	13
College	29	15	34	22

A question must be raised on just how much these attitudes toward the police are rooted in racial antagonisms and how much these attitudes derive from fear of crime itself. The entire sample was asked who would be more likely to commit a crime against them, a black or a white person (see Table 74).

City-wide, a majority replied that it could be a person of either race or that they were not sure. But among those willing to choose, sight unseen, a black or white potential assailant, five times as many named a black as a white. The only major exception could be found on Staten Island, where blacks represent only a few percentage points of the total population, making it unlikely for a black to commit a crime against them personally. It also is no surprise to find that blacks said blacks are more likely to assail them. But, once again, among

TABLE 73

PERCEPTION OF POLICE TREATMENT OF BLACKS: NON-JEWISH WHITES

	Use Brutality %	Too Lenient %	Fair %	Not Sure %
Total Jewish	18	23	42	17
21 to 34	28	20	34	18
35 to 49	24	20	34	22
50 and over	5	27	53	15
8th grade	-	38	46	16
High school	11	27	49	13
College	29	15	34	22
Total Blacks	48	8	24	20
21 to 34	58	6	40	16
35 to 49	45	7	24	24
50 and over	32	14	34	19
8th grade	38	11	29	22
High school	49	7	24	20
College	56	6	21	17
Total Non-Jewish White	22	18	39	21
21-34	32	15	33	20
35-49	18	18	40	24
50 and over	9	22	48	21
No college	19	20	40	21
Some college	29	13	37	21

the nonblack population, Jews led in expecting blacks to commit crimes against them. On a borough-by-borough basis, Manhattan, with the heaviest proportion of blacks, the Bronx, and Brooklyn all singled out blacks as the ones more likely to be committers of crimes, more even than Queens.

A Jewish doctor in Manhattan expressed his reasoning this way: "Well, Negroes are more prone to commit crimes. They have a higher crime rate in their own neighborhoods.

HOW BLACKS ARE PERCEIVED 87

TABLE 74

BLACK/WHITE MORE LIKELY TO COMMIT
CRIME AGAINST YOU: CITY-WIDE

	Black %	White %	Depends[a] %	No Diff[a] %	Not Sure %
Total City	24	5	20	33	18
Jewish	28	2	16	35	19
Black	35	10	24	18	13
White Catholic	18	6	18	38	20
Puerto Rican	16	2	22	36	24
White Protestant	18	4	30	38	10
Manhattan	25	2	19	36	18
Bronx	22	4	26	30	18
Queens	19	5	24	34	18
Brooklyn	28	6	16	32	18
Richmond	5	28	2	53	12

[a] Volunteered response.

So I can only conclude that I am more likely to be robbed or beaten by a Negro." A 36-year-old man who earns $17,000 a year in advertising and lives in Queens said, "We have some Negroes in our neighborhood and they are much more likely to commit crimes than the whites who live here."

Of course, only a minority of the Jewish group singled out blacks or whites as likely criminal assailants. A Brooklyn man put it this way: "The lower socio-economic groups are more apt to commit a crime. Race is purely incidental." A 27-year-old housewife in Queens, whose husband earns $22,000 a year, said, "I don't think only Negroes do bad things. Whites do their share but you don't hear about it as much."

A statistical summary of the volunteered remarks of the Jewish group on the question of which race might be more likely to commit a crime against them is shown in Table 75.

Jews and non-Jewish whites divided by age and education on this question as shown in Table 76.

Younger and college-educated Jews differed significantly from older, lesser educated Jews. Similarly, younger and college educated non-Jewish whites were less likely to see the

TABLE 75

FEELINGS BEHIND VIEWS ON WHO MORE LIKELY TO COMMIT CRIME: JEWS

	Total Jewish %
Why Blacks More Likely	**32**
They commit most of the crimes	13
It's happened to me	5
Most blacks live poorly	4
Resentment of whites	4
Impression from news media	3
Many dope addicts are black	3
Why Whites More Likely	**2**
Live in white area	2
Why Depends	**68**
Race isn't the determinant	45
Depends where crime occurs	11
Depends on individual	7
Depends on situation	3
Depends on type of crime	1
Black crimes get more publicity	1
Not Sure	**8**

color of crime as black than older and less educated non-Jewish whites. However, it should be noted that younger and college-educated Jews tended to believe blacks more likely to commit a crime than their counterparts among non-Jewish whites.

For the blacks, the reasoning was relatively simple. As a 32-year-old unemployed black woman in the Jamaica section of Queens said, "In this neighborhood there are no whites to commit the crime. If this was a different neighborhood, it would be a different story, you can bet your life on that." In the Bedford-Stuyvesant section, a 54-year-old laborer earning $6,500 a year explained, "Blacks and white are both criminals. It just depends on who happens to be around when something is

HOW BLACKS ARE PERCEIVED

TABLE 76

BLACK/WHITE MORE LIKELY TO COMMIT A CRIME AGAINST YOU: JEWS AND NON-JEWISH WHITES

	Black %	White %	Depends %	No Diff[a] %	Not Sure %
Total Jewish	28	2	16	35	19
21 to 34	22	4	16	38	20
35 to 49	33	3	13	32	19
50 and over	31	b	18	36	15
8th grade	35	1	19	33	12
High school	30	1	16	33	20
College	25	3	15	38	19
Total Non-Jewish Whites	17	4	21	38	20
21 to 34	15	4	26	33	22
35 to 49	20	3	19	38	20
50 and over	19	5	16	45	15
No college	17	3	21	38	21
Some college	20	7	21	39	13

[a] Volunteered response.
[b] Less than 0.5 percent.

committed against you." A skilled laborer in Harlem said, "Look, I live in an all-black area. There are more blacks here than anywhere else in the city. No white person comes to Harlem to commit crimes, at least the ones you can see. My so-called soul brother may rob me or beat me. 'Whitey' kills me in other ways. He don't need to come up here in person to do it with crime."

A summary of black remarks about crime is shown in Table 77.

It must be pointed out that a majority of each group are rational enough to qualify their feelings voluntarily, by stating that any particular crime might be committed by a person of any race, creed, color, or national origin.

TABLE 77

FEELINGS BEHIND VIEWS ON WHO MORE LIKELY
TO COMMIT CRIME: BLACKS

	Total Blacks[a] %
Why Blacks More Likely	
Most crimes are committed by blacks	14
Black communities have addicts who need money	5
Higher black unemployment rate	4
Blacks don't respect each other and property	4
Blacks poorer, more deprived	2
Robbed, mugged by a black myself	2
Idle black teenagers, troublemakers	1
Most petty crimes committed by blacks	1
Why Whites More Likely	
Black wouldn't attack a black brother	2
Never had trouble with my own people	2
Whites heartless, dislike blacks	2
Most economic crimes committed by whites	1
Why Depends	
Anybody can commit a crime	27
Depends on which community you are in	18
Depends on circumstances	4
Depends on type of crime	2
Not Sure	

[a] Adds to more than 100 percent as some respondents volunteered more than one response.

However, with blacks careful to point out that in their neighborhoods the crimes are highly unlikely to be white-committed, and many whites, particularly in the Jewish group, saying blacks are more likely to commit a crime against them, there is substantial feeling in New York that the criminal tends to be black.

HOW BLACKS ARE PERCEIVED

TABLE 78

UPSET IN CERTAIN SITUATIONS

	Jewish %	Non-Jewish Whites %	Non-Jewish White "Backlash" %
Upset if:			
1. Law passed giving blacks preference over whites in certain jobs	84	71	88
2. City increased money given to blacks on welfare	74	63	83
3. Board of Education decided to bus white children from your neighborhood into schools in black areas	72	56	82
4. Board of Education decided to bus black children into your neighborhood schools	46	37	56
5. More blacks moved into this neighborhood	56	39	66

CONCERN IN CERTAIN SITUATIONS

In addition to the roster of questions asked of all groups to measure gaps in perception, communication, and understanding of the lot of black people in New York City, whites were also asked a series of questions designed to find out some of their apprehensions.

TABLE 79

UPSET IN CERTAIN SITUATIONS: JEWS AND
NON-JEWISH WHITES BY AGE AND EDUCATION

	1 Upset %	2 Upset %	3 Upset %	4[a] Upset %
Total Jewish	84	74	72	46
21-34	85	68	73	45
35-49	77	73	74	48
50 and over	88	81	71	46
8th grade	90	81	69	52
High school	86	78	77	49
College	79	69	70	42
Total Non-Jewish Whites	71	63	56	37
21-34	69	57	53	35
35-49	69	64	56	36
50 and over	80	72	62	44
No college	67	63	55	39
Some college	83	65	60	34

[a] Situations (1, 2, 3, 4) are numbered to correspond with description in Table 78. Situation 5 breakdown by age and education appears in Table 80.

One of these series dealt with whether or not the Jewish group, the non-Jewish whites, and the special "backlash" sample group would be upset if certain things happened (see Tables 78 and 79).

All three groups registered a high percentage of "upset" responses if a law were passed giving blacks preference over whites in certain jobs. Especially high proportions of the non-Jewish white "backlash" sample said they would be upset. Given the results already described on perceived discrimination against blacks in specific situations, this result is not surprising.

Preferential treatment for blacks in New York City by mid-1969 would unquestionably meet with overwhelming and widespread white resistance and resentment.

HOW BLACKS ARE PERCEIVED 93

A similarly high percentage of "upset" responses was recorded when whites were asked how they would feel if the city increased the money given to blacks on welfare. More appears on the subject of welfare in another chapter.

Jews and non-Jewish whites in the special "backlash" sample said they would be particularly upset if the Board of Education decided to bus white children from their neighborhood into schools in black areas. Fewer non-Jewish whites would be upset, although a majority of 56 percent would still feel that way.

The opposite policy, "if the Board of Education decided to bus black children into your neighborhood schools," evoked a majority reply of "upset" from the special anti-Civilian Review Board area, but less than a majority (46 percent), of "upset" responses among the Jews and barely over a third (37 percent) of "upset" responses from non-Jewish whites.

However, the idea of more blacks moving into the neighborhood received a majority of "upset" responses from Jews (56 percent) and an even higher 66 percent from the special non-Jewish white "backlash" sample. But the non-Jewish white regular sample reacted with 17 percentage points fewer "upset" responses than did the Jewish sample. The division within the Jewish community on the question is shown in Table 80.

Clearly, Bronx and Brooklyn Jews took quite a different attitude on this issue than did Manhattan and Queens Jews. Orthodox Jews were most concerned with blacks moving into their neighborhoods. Again, there was a sharp split between the under-35 and the over-50 Jews, as there was between the college educated and the least well educated, and those practicing the Jewish faith and those who are not affiliated.

As Bronx Jews who live in areas rather heavily inundated by recently arrived blacks and Puerto Ricans pointed out in their interviews, affluent Jews who live in expensive apartments in Manhattan do not have to worry about the likelihood of a large-scale black influx. Nonetheless, the results show that among young people and those with a college education, there is an almost completely consistent pattern of far greater tolerance than among their elders and those with less education in the Jewish group. Indeed, the younger members of the non-Jewish white group also tend to show greater tolerance. Judged on the basis of the "upset if" questions, the position of the college educated in this group is more ambiguous. However, on the crucial questions of whether they would be upset if more blacks moved into the neighborhood, the college educated showed a significantly lower "upset" response than those with no college education, 33 percent compared to 41 percent.

TABLE 80

UPSET IF MORE BLACKS MOVED INTO NEIGHBORHOOD: JEWS AND NON-JEWISH WHITES

	Upset %	Not Upset %	Not Sure %
Total Jewish	56	30	14
Manhattan	39	52	9
Bronx	70	27	3
Queens	49	43	8
Brooklyn	63	24	13
Orthodox	74	16	10
Conservative	66	24	10
Reform	55	37	8
Non-affiliated	29	43	28
21-34	42	47	11
35-49	53	36	11
50+	67	25	8
8th grade	71	21	8
High school	65	27	8
College	43	46	11
Total Non-Jewish Whites	39	53	6
21-34	36	58	7
35-49	39	54	7
50+	46	47	6
No college	41	50	7
Some college	33	63	4

TABLE 81

PERSONAL CONCERN OVER CONTACT WITH BLACKS: WHITE CITY-WIDE AND NATIONAL

Concerned if:	Jewish %	Non-Jewish Whites %	Non-Jewish White "Backlash" %	July 1967 National White Voters %
Black sat next to you at lunch counter	1	1	2	12
Black sat next to you at movie theater	2	2	5	14
Black used same public restroom	2	2	4	14
Your child brought black child home to supper	16	17	28	34
Walking along street, black person crossed over, began walking toward you	20	11	18	--
Black family moved next door	22	19	37	40
Close friend, relative married a black	63	44	67	77
Your teenage daughter dated a black	76	56	83	89

The nonblack cross-section of New York was asked about personal concern over specific kinds of contact with blacks.

On the whole, New York whites showed less concern in 1969 than the American public did in 1967. By and large, people who live in the special "backlash" sample areas were more concerned about contact with blacks than either the Jewish or non-Jewish white groups. However, on one count, "concerned if walking along the street, a black person crossed over and began walking toward you," Jews expressed more concern than the others. A significant difference between Jews and other whites appeared in answers to a question about concern over a close friend or a relative marrying a black; 63 percent of the Jews expressed concern, compared with a minority of 44 percent of the non-Jewish whites. (It should be pointed out, though, that the figure for the Italians on this question was 55 percent "concerned" and for the Irish an even higher 59 percent "concerned".) Further, 76 percent of the Jewish group said it would be concerned if a teen-age daughter dated a black, compared with a much lower 56 percent among the non-Jewish whites.

Table 82 breaks down the Jews and non-Jewish whites by age and education on the subject of concern over a close friend or relative marrying a black. The responses show a very marked difference between the young and college educated and the older and less educated members of both groups.

Although younger and college-educated Jews admitted greater concern than their counterparts among non-Jewish whites, they showed a good deal less concern than older and less educated Jews.

One can only conclude that the Jewish group, like the special non-Jewish white sample, is rather deeply concerned with the kind of personal contact with blacks that might lead to social relations, particularly ultimately with intermarriage. Needless to say, so are the non-Jewish whites, but certainly to a much lesser extent. It should also be noted that although younger and college-educated Jews showed more concern than their counterparts among non-Jewish whites, they showed significantly less than their elders and the less well educated.

STEREOTYPES ABOUT BLACKS

The white groups in the sample were given a series of stereotypes about blacks and asked if they tended to agree

TABLE 82

CONCERNED IF CLOSE FRIEND OR RELATIVE
MARRIED A BLACK: JEWS AND NON-JEWISH WHITES

	Concerned %	Not Concerned %	Not Sure %
Total Jewish	63	29	8
21 to 34	47	42	11
35 to 49	66	25	9
50 and over	76	20	4
8th grade	71	24	5
High school	61	34	5
College	51	33	16
Total Non-Jewish Whites	44	45	11
21 to 34	36	57	7
35 to 49	43	37	20
50 and over	56	34	10
No college	46	42	12
Some college	36	52	12

or disagree with each. The results appear in Table 83. Age and education breakdowns for the answers to each of these questions for Jews and non-Jewish whites are shown in Tables 84, 87, and 88.

The stereotypes about blacks were most believed by whites living in the areas which voted over 80 percent against the Civilian Review Board, next most by the Jews, and least by the non-Jewish whites.

Over 40 percent of the Jews felt that blacks tend to breed more crime and have looser morals than whites, compared with roughly 3 in 10 among the non-Jewish whites and close to 50 percent of the white "backlash" sample. Similarly, approximately 3 in 10 Jews tended to believe that blacks care less for the family than whites, want to live off a hand-out, and just like to stir up trouble, compared with almost half that number among the non-Jewish whites.

TABLE 83

STEREOTYPES OF BLACKS: CITY-WIDE AND NATIONAL

	Jewish %	Non-Jewish Whites %	Non-Jewish White "Backlash" %	July 1967 National White Voters %
Agree that blacks:				
1. Have less ambition than whites	43	32	54	70
2. Have looser morals than whites	42	28	48	34
3. Breed more crime	41	32	48	32
4. Care less for the family than whites	32	19	34	46
5. Want to live off a hand-out	30	17	43	52
6. Just like to stir up trouble	27	14	34	--
7. Have less native intelligence than whites	22	13	33	46
8. Smell different	22	16	29	59
9. Keep untidy homes	21	16	27	46

TABLE 84

STEREOTYPES OF BLACKS: JEWS AND NON-JEWISH WHITES
BY AGE AND EDUCATION

	2[a] Agree %	4 Agree %	5 Agree %	6 Agree %	7 Agree %	8 Agree %	9 Agree %
Total Jewish	42	32	30	27	22	22	21
21-34	33	28	20	27	14	19	15
35-49	43	29	26	34	15	21	16
50 and over	50	39	40	49	34	25	28
8th grade	58	39	54	61	36	25	39
High school	48	39	32	45	28	26	24
College	33	25	21	24	13	18	13
Total Non-Jewish Whites	28	19	17	14	13	16	16
21-34	28	16	14	14	12	16	16
35-49	25	18	13	11	12	14	13
50 and over	35	25	28	20	17	18	22
No college	29	18	19	17	14	17	17
Some college	26	21	12	6	10	13	15

[a] Stereotypes (2, 4, 5, 6, 7, 8, 9) are numbered to correspond with description in Table 83. Stereotype 1 breakdown appears in Table 87, stereotype 3 breakdown in Table 88.

TABLE 85

BLACKS WANT TO LIVE OFF A HANDOUT:
"BACKLASH" WHITES

	Agree %	Disagree %	Not Sure %
Total Non-Jewish White "Backlash"	43	33	24
Catholic	44	33	23
Non-Catholic	39	33	28
Italian	48	25	27
Irish	42	35	23
21-34	38	42	20
35-49	44	33	23
50+	47	23	30
No college	48	26	26
Some college	22	61	17
Skilled labor	51	24	25
Unskilled labor	50	24	26
Professional, executive	22	53	25
White collar	43	30	27

The "backlash" non-Jewish white sample group appeared to give particular credence to the oft-repeated claim that blacks just want to live off a handout. The breakdown of this group by religion, ethnic group, age, education, and type of work shows some interesting patterns in New York City.

It is evident as Table 85 shows, that Catholics more than non-Catholics, Italians more than Irish, older more than younger people, those with no college education more than those with college training, and those who are either skilled or unskilled, laborers more than professional, executive, or white collar workers adhered to this stereotype.

But even sharper differences emerged when the same non-Jewish white "backlash" sample group is broken down by age, education, and other factors on the proposition that blacks have less native intelligence than whites.

TABLE 86

BLACKS HAVE LESS NATIVE INTELLIGENCE: "BACKLASH" WHITES

	Agree %	Disagree %	Not Sure %
Total Non-Jewish White "Backlash"	33	42	25
Catholic	33	42	25
Non-Catholic	32	42	26
Italian	42	25	33
Irish	27	56	17
21-34	25	57	18
35-49	36	39	25
50+	40	28	32
No college	35	36	29
Some college	24	68	8
Belong to union	33	41	26
Skilled labor	34	39	27
Unskilled labor	40	35	25

On this stereotype, Italians tended to believe the proposition by 42 percent to 25 percent, while the Irish denied it by 56 percent to 27 percent. The under-35 age group denied it by 57 percent to 25 percent, but the over-50 age group believed it by 40 percent to 28 percent. Those with some college education disagreed with the proposition by 68 percent to 24 percent.

The Jewish community, for its part, also had sharp deviations in its own ranks on some of the stereotypes. For example, take the breakdown on the question of whether blacks breeding more crime than whites (data shown in Table 87).

Manhattan and Queens Jews made estimates on this stereotype sharply different from the estimates of Brooklyn Jews. Similarly, Orthodox Jews believed most strongly that blacks

TABLE 87

BLACKS BREED MORE CRIME: JEWS AND NON-JEWISH WHITES

	Agree %	Disagree %	Not Sure %
Total Jewish	41	36	23
Manhattan	35	49	16
Bronx	47	42	11
Queens	34	41	25
Brooklyn	47	21	32
Orthodox	59	17	24
Conservative	47	29	24
Reform	43	31	26
Non-affiliated	15	67	18
21-34	31	50	19
35-49	46	32	22
50+	49	25	26
8th grade	61	13	26
High school	46	28	26
College	32	49	19
Total Non-Jewish Whites	32	46	22
21-34	31	47	20
35-49	27	48	24
50+	38	37	24
No college	32	43	24
Some college	32	49	17

TABLE 88

BLACKS TEND TO HAVE LESS AMBITION THAN WHITES: JEWS AND NON-JEWISH WHITES

	Agree %	Disagree %	Not Sure %
Total Jewish	<u>43</u>	<u>44</u>	<u>13</u>
Manhattan	23	68	9
Bronx	51	42	7
Queens	42	44	14
Brooklyn	51	31	18
Orthodox	57	30	13
Conservative	50	32	18
Reform	50	38	12
Non-affiliated	15	76	9
21-34	36	53	11
35-49	34	48	18
50+	54	33	13
8th grade	58	29	13
High school	50	34	16
College	33	56	11
Total Non-Jewish Whites	<u>31</u>	<u>52</u>	<u>16</u>
21-34	27	57	16
35-49	27	55	17
50+	44	41	15
No college	32	50	17
Some college	29	59	13

tend to breed crime, and non-affiliated Jews believed this stereotype least of all. Again, there is a sharp split between the under-35 age group, which denied the proposition by 50 percent to 31 percent, compared with those aged 50 and over, who accepted it by 49 percent to 25 percent. And too, there is a comparable split between the eighth-grade-educated Jews, who felt that blacks breed crime by 61 percent to 13 percent, and the college-educated group, who denied it by 49 percent to 32 percent.

Even sharper splits can be observed on the stereotype that blacks tend to have less ambition than whites; the responses of Jews and non-Jewish whites on this stereotype are summarized in Table 88.

Once more, the answers showed the contrast between Manhattan and Queens Jews and those in the Bronx and Brooklyn. Orthodox Jews, true to the pattern already observed, tended to believe the stereotype more than others, while non-affiliated Jews disagreed with it. The split by age is dramatic: the 21-34 group denied the charge by 53 to 36 percent, but the over-50 group believed it by 54 to 33 percent. The education split polarizes the Jewish group even more: Jews with eighth-grade education tended to believe it 58 to 29 percent, but the group of college educated denied it 56 to 33 percent.

Thus there is a significant difference between younger and older Jews and between college-educated and less educated Jews in their responses on all of the stereotypes. The age difference is particularly marked between the group aged 21 to 34 and the 50-and-over group. Among non-Jewish whites the age and education divisions are less marked, though on most of the stereotypes differences emerged. Among non-Jewish whites those 21 to 34 years old and those 35 to 49 years old tended to give similar responses, while those over 50 tended far more often to accept the stereotypes. In general, the college educated agreed with the stereotypes less often than those with no college education.

BLACK ANTI-SEMITISM

The Jewish group was tested on a proposition that was not put to any of the other groups: "Blacks tend to be anti-Semitic." They were asked if they agree or disagree with that statement; the results are shown in Table 89.

TABLE 89

BLACKS TEND TO BE ANTI-SEMITIC: JEWS

	Agree %	Disagree %	Not Sure %
Total Jewish	38	41	21
Manhattan	23	61	16
Bronx	48	42	10
Queens	26	49	25
Brooklyn	49	23	28
Orthodox	50	26	24
Conservative	46	31	23
Reform	40	37	23
Non-affiliated	16	70	14
21-34	27	48	25
35-49	34	48	18
50+	49	30	21
8th grade	61	14	25
High school	45	34	21
College	24	54	22

By a narrow 41 to 38 percent margin, the Jews in New York City disagreed with the proposition. The statement was emphatically denied by Manhattan and Queens Jews, but was solidly believed by Brooklyn Jews. Orthodox Jews believed it 50 to 26 percent, while Reform Jews went along with it by a narrow 40 to 37 percent. Again, Jews who do not feel formally affiliated with one or another branch of their religion clearly did not believe blacks tend to be anti-Semitic. This group's position explains the over-all disagreement with the statement.

The breakdown by age showed that young Jews denied the proposition 48 to 27 percent, but older Jews believed it by 49 to 30 percent. As in other breakdowns, the split by education is most dramatic: those Jewish people with an eighth-grade education or less believed that blacks are anti-Semitic by a large 61-14 percent margin, while those Jews with a college education denied it by 54 to 24 percent.

It is perfectly clear that by mid-1969 in New York City, much of the city's traditionally accepted feeling for blacks as underdogs had eroded and even disappeared. Perhaps some of the groups in the city had always harbored anti-black sentiment.

Most affected, clearly, have been Jews who live in Brooklyn, those who are Orthodox in their religion, those over 50 years of age, and those with the least education. They tended to deny that discrimination against blacks takes place, they tended to believe many of the stereotypes about blacks, such as that they "breed crime," "don't care for their families as whites do," "have less ambition than whites," and "tend to be anti-Semitic."

But pitted against these Jewish groups are other Jews who hold almost opposite views. In fact, the split in the Jewish community is fully as great as the gap between Jews and blacks, as groups in the aggregate. The young, the educated, those who do not conform to one of the three major divisions of the Jewish religion, those who live in Manhattan and in Queens, all tended to disagree with their co-religionists on the matter of race.

Quite similar divisions can be observed among the white Catholic groups, where the young, the educated, and those who live in Manhattan held fewer negative views about blacks than their older, less well educated brethren who live in the Bronx, Brooklyn, and Staten Island.

In the beginning of this analysis we said there were two New Yorks--one the center of communications, commerce, and corporate decision making, the other, the New York in which some 7,000,000 people live. The truth is that the second New York itself is becoming two New Yorks in a very profound sense. The city has taken on many of the overtones of the two Americas which exist beyond the Hudson River, with the blacks, the young, and the college educated on one side and the older and the less educated on the other. Racial attitudes are a central reason for the division.

One difference, though, is that most of the rest of America is white Protestant, and in New York City white Protestants are a minority. And in the country as a whole, WASPs tend to be less sympathetic to the blacks than other groups, while in New York City the opposite is true. The WASPs tend to be far more sympathetic to the blacks than either the Jews or the Catholics.

Another difference is New York's ethnic diversity. New York is a majority of minorities; and it has been able to hold together because these minorities have accepted an unwritten but well understood rule that each must respect the other. This rule has been strained in the case of attitudes toward blacks. A basic question is whether minorities can hold views as negative about blacks without examining attitudes toward themselves as minorities. This would apply especially to the Jewish minority, attitudes toward whom are examined in the following chapter.

CHAPTER 4 HOW JEWS ARE PERCEIVED

Any confrontation must have two groups in conflict. The preceding Chapter showed how Jews and non-Jewish whites perceive blacks and how blacks look at themselves. This Chapter centers on non-Jewish white and black attitudes toward New York's Jewish community--the other major group in the confrontation. It also examines how the Jewish community views non-Jewish white and black attitudes toward Jews.

POSITIVE AND NEGATIVE STEREOTYPES

The study included a roster of 10 positive and 10 negative stereotypes about Jews and asked blacks and non-Jewish whites whether they agree or disagree with each. From responses to this battery of questions the relative levels of anti-Jewish feeling among key groups in the city can be determined.

However, an additional experiment was conducted among the Jewish people themselves. Each Jew in the sample was asked to give his estimate on how he thought most non-Jewish whites would feel about precisely the same items. It is therefore possible in this study to find out not only how others in New York City see Jews, but also to compare the level of pro-Jewish or anti-Jewish sentiment with what Jewish people think it is.

Table 90 summarizes all these attitudes together. Columns 1 and 2 show Jewish estimates of how non-Jewish whites and blacks feel on each item; Columns 1 through 7 report on what non-Jewish white, black, Puerto Rican, and white Protestant perceptions of Jews actually are. Columns 8 and 9 list the gaps between Jewish perception and black attitudes and Jewish perception and non-Jewish white attitudes.

Usually when attitudes especially black attitudes, toward Jews are discussed, the emphasis is placed on the negative rather than the positive side. This study attempts to look at both sides. As will be made clear, blacks when surveyed

TABLE 90

STEREOTYPES OF JEWS

	Jews, Estimate Non-Jew. Whites %	Jews, Estimate Blacks %	Total Non-Jew. Whites %	Non-Jew. Black %	White Cath. %	Puerto Rican %	White Prot. %	Gap Blacks %	Whites %
POSITIVE:									
Raise Their Children to Accomplish Something in World									
Agree	82	65	86	84	83	59	89	-19	-4
Disagree	7	14	4	6	4	12	5		
Not sure	11	21	10	10	13	29	6		
Suffered from Persecution Through the Centuries									
Agree	65	47	76	72	73	50	82	-25	-11
Disagree	26	40	14	16	12	21	9		
Not sure	9	13	10	12	15	29	9		
Supported Minority Rights More Than Other Whites									
Agree	64	44	56	59	50	26	56	-15	+8
Disagree	21	40	14	17	17	28	19		
Not sure	15	16	30	24	33	46	25		
Always Supported Civil Rights for Blacks									
Agree	64	38	51	46	48	22	56	-8	+13
Disagree	15	42	16	22	11	22	17		
Not sure	21	20	33	32	41	56	27		
Give Lot of Money to Good Causes									
Agree	55	37	60	49	55	25	68	-12	-5
Disagree	20	39	9	21	8	26	11		
Not sure	25	24	31	30	37	49	21		
In Professions More Because Study Harder in School									
Agree	55	40	57	63	54	29	61	-23	-2
Disagree	22	34	20	19	19	35	22		
Not sure	23	26	23	18	27	36	17		
Stick with Own No More Than Other Groups									
Agree	54	40	64	48	64	35	63	-8	-10
Disagree	25	39	25	35	25	33	27		
Not sure	21	21	11	17	11	32	10		

(continued)

TABLE 90 (Continued)

	Jews, Estimate Non-Jew. Whites %	Blacks %	Total Non-Jew. Whites %	Black %	White Cath. %	Puerto Rican %	White Prot. %	Gaps Between Jews, Estimate and Views of: Blacks %	Whites %
POSITIVE: (continued)									
Same People Who Keep Jews Down Also Keep Blacks Down									
Agree	49	39	41	70	33	26	52	-31	+8
Disagree	21	35	26	12	31	29	19		
Not sure	30	26	33	18	36	45	29		
As Honest As Other Businessmen									
Agree	48	23	73	36	71	44	77	-13	-25
Disagree	34	60	16	44	17	26	13		
Not sure	18	17	11	20	12	30	10		
Have to Work Harder Because Discriminated Against									
Agree	35	24	25	42	23	12	28	-18	+10
Disagree	44	55	53	36	54	36	52		
Not sure	21	21	22	22	23	52	20		
NEGATIVE:									
Most Slum Lords Are Jewish									
Agree	55	80	34	73	31	50	41	+7	+21
Disagree	27	9	21	8	21	12	16		
Not sure	18	11	45	19	48	38	43		
Jews Are Richer Than Other People									
Agree	53	78	36	69	36	50	36	+9	+17
Disagree	31	13	44	16	41	25	48		
Not sure	16	9	20	15	23	25	16		
Jews More a Race Than a Religion									
Agree	44	54	32	57	34	32	29	-3	+12
Disagree	34	24	53	26	49	32	60		
Not sure	22	22	15	17	17	36	11		
Jews Are Irritating Because Too Aggressive									
Agree	43	54	21	49	20	22	23	+5	+22
Disagree	35	28	59	28	60	43	58		
Not sure	22	18	20	23	20	35	19		

	Jews, Estimate Non-Jew.		Total Non-Jew.	Black	White Cath.	Puerto Rican	White Prot.	Gaps Between Jews, Estimate and Views of:	
	Whites %	Blacks %	Whites %	%	%	%	%	Blacks %	Whites %
NEGATIVE: (continued)									
Between Money and People, Jews Will Choose Money									
Agree	40	59	23	71	25	37	20	-12	+17
Disagree	37	20	51	11	47	22	57		
Not sure	23	21	26	18	28	41	23		
Jewish Businessmen Will Try to Put Over a Shady Deal on You									
Agree	40	66	17	62	17	29	17	+4	+23
Disagree	41	15	66	17	63	30	72		
Not sure	19	19	17	21	20	41	11		
Too Ambitious for Their Own Good									
Agree	40	54	11	39	12	28	9	+15	+29
Disagree	38	24	72	37	69	32	77		
Not sure	22	22	17	24	19	40	14		
Feel Superior to Other Groups									
Agree	40	57	27	53	30	35	22	+4	+13
Disagree	38	22	50	22	50	28	50		
Not sure	22	21	23	25	20	37	28		
Stick to Their Own and Never Give Outsider a Break									
Agree	35	54	20	49	21	35	17	+5	+15
Disagree	45	25	67	31	65	35	71		
Not sure	20	21	13	20	14	30	12		
More Loyal to Israel Than to America									
Agree	28	37	18	52	23	23	11	-15	+10
Disagree	44	29	57	21	52	32	64		
Not sure	28	34	25	27	25	45	25		

showed some real hostility toward Jews. However, they displayed some markedly positive views about Jews as well.

On the positive stereotype items about Jews, the most striking finding is that the Jewish group underestimated the views blacks hold about them in all of the ten items. Consistently higher percentages of blacks answered favorably about Jews here than the Jewish group estimated they would.

The same is not true of Jewish estimates of non-Jewish white attitudes. In four out of ten favorable items, Jews tended to overestimate the agreement of non-Jewish whites, although in six out of ten they underestimated.

Easily the least positive views of Jews were held not by black people in New York, but by Puerto Ricans, while white Protestants were the most positive.

Specifically, on the separate items, the biggest gap between Jewish estimates of black attitudes and black attitudes themselves appears on the item, "The same people who keep Jews down also keep blacks down." Jews estimated that blacks would agree with that statement by only a slim 39-35 percent. In fact, blacks hold this view by a lopsided 70-12 percent margin, or 31 percentage points over the way Jews thought blacks feel. By contrast, on this same statement, Jews tended to overestimate the feelings of non-Jewish whites. The Jewish group guessed that the non-Jewish whites would come out at 49-21 percent in agreement. In fact, the non-Jewish whites divided 41-26 percent in agreement, or 8 percentage points below where Jews thought they would.

It is apparent that the traditional bond of minorities joining together in the face of a common adversary provides a potential common bond between Jews and blacks, at least in the view of the blacks. They were overwhelmingly convinced that the same people who are anti-Semitic are also anti-black. Although a majority of white Protestants also shared this view, white Catholics and Puerto Ricans clearly did not. White Catholics agreed with the statement by only 33-31 percent and Puerto Ricans disagreed by 29-26 percent, although sizable numbers of both groups were not able to make a judgment.

Another sizable gap exists in the answers to the statement, "Jews have suffered from persecution through the centuries." By only a slim 47-40 percent, Jews themselves estimated that blacks would agree with it. However, a much higher 72-16 percent majority of blacks agreed with the claim, amounting to a gap of 25 percentage points between Jewish estimates and the views expressed by blacks. Jews also underestimated the attitudes of non-Jewish whites, expecting them to agree with the statement by 65-26 percent. Actually, the non-Jewish whites agreed with it by 76-14 percent, amounting to a gap of 11 percentage points. Most reluctant to accept the fact of past Jewish persecution were the Puerto Ricans, who agreed by only 50-21 percent.

There is a clear recognition among blacks in New York of the past suffering of the Jews. This recognition offers a possible base for more understanding between Jews and blacks.

Still another wide gap between Jewish expectations and black attitudes exists over the statement that "Jews are in the professions more because they study harder in school." Jews estimated that blacks would agree with that view by only 40-34 percent. In fact, blacks agreed with it by a decisive 63-19 percent, or 23 points higher than Jews believed it to be. Indeed blacks, more than any other single group in the population of New York City, believed that Jews work harder to succeed in the professions. The Jewish group was more accurate in its assessment of how non-Jewish whites feel, estimating they would divide 55-22 percent favorable. The results show that non-Jewish whites were 57-20 percent in agreement, a gap of only two percentage points over the Jewish estimate. However, the Puerto Rican group denied the validity of the statement by a 35-29 percent margin.

Another gap exists over the statement that "the Jews raise their children to accomplish something in the world." The Jewish group expected widespread black acceptance of this claim by 65-14 percent. However, blacks far exceeded this estimate, agreeing with the statement by 84-6 percent, or 19 percentage points over what Jews thought it would be. Again, Jews were more realistic about non-Jewish white attitudes, which came in at an even higher 86-4 percent agreement. Once more, however, Puerto Ricans trailed behind, supporting the belief by a much lower 59-12 percent margin.

The statement, "Jews have to work harder because they are discriminated against," produced one of the most interesting results. Jews themselves did not expect others to agree with this statement. By 55 to 24 percent, they thought that blacks would disagree with it. By a lesser 44-35 percent they thought non-Jewish whites would disagree with it. In fact, the Jews overestimated the non-Jewish whites, who weighed in with a much higher 53-25 percent disagreement, a gap of 10 percentage points in the agreement column. Puerto Ricans disagreed by 36-12 percent, although 52 percent were not sure.

But by a slim 42-36 percent margin, blacks actually agreed with the statement--a result 18 percentage points above what Jews expected them to feel. In fact, blacks were the only group in the population of New York City who believed that Jews work harder because they are discriminated against.

Again, it is apparent that there ia a potential source of black-Jewish empathy in the response blacks gave on the question of how hard Jews have to work to overcome discrimination. Clearly, however, in today's climate, the Jewish community has little sense that blacks feel this way.

Jewish assessments of both blacks and non-Jewish whites clearly were awry over the statement, "Jews have supported minority rights more than other whites." By only a narrow 44-40 percent, Jews expected blacks to agree. But, in fact, blacks agreed with the statement by a much more lopsided 59-17 percent. The reverse pattern appears among non-Jewish whites. By 64-21 percent, Jews expected that group to agree with their support of minority rights. Non-Jewish whites did agree, but by a lower 56-14 percent, or eight percentage points below Jewish expectations of them. Again by 28-26 percent, Puerto Ricans disagreed with the statement, albeit with 46 percent of them expressing no view.

A similar pattern is evident over the statement, "Jews have always supported civil rights for blacks." Jews expected non-Jewish whites to agree with this by a wide 64-15 percent. They did agree, but by a somewhat lesser 51-16 percent, or 13 points less than the Jewish estimate. On the other hand, Jews expected that blacks would disagree that they had helped the civil rights cause by 42-38 percent. But blacks agreed with the statement by a convincing 46-22 percent, less than was the case among the non-Jewish whites, but still 8 percentage points higher than Jews believed.

Another area of Jewish underestimation emerges over the statement, "Jews give a lot of money to good causes." The Jewish group expected non-Jewish whites to agree by 55-20 percent, but they agreed by a larger 60-9 percent. Jews expected blacks to disagree that they are generous with their money by 39-37 percent. However, blacks agreed with the statement 49-21 percent, not as high as non-Jewish whites, but considerably better than Puerto Ricans, who disagreed by 26-25 percent.

A comparable pattern is evident over the statement, "Jews stick with their own no more than other groups." Jews expected non-Jewish whites to agree with that claim by 54-25 percent, but in reality they agreed by 64-25 percent, 10 percentage points higher. Jews thought that blacks would be closely divided, agreeing by a slim 40-39 percent. However, blacks agreed with the statement by a much wider 48-35 percent. Puerto Ricans, in contrast, agreed by only 35-33 percent.

The Jewish group was cautious in its expectation of non-Jewish white attitudes on the statement, "Jews are as honest as other businessmen." They expected non-Jewish whites to agree by 48-34 percent, less than a majority, In fact, non-Jewish whites agreed overwhelmingly by a thumping 73-16 percent, a 25 percentage point underestimation by the Jewish group.

In the case of blacks, Jews were extremely doubtful, estimating by 60-23 percent that the blacks would come down on the negative side of the question. The facts show that Jewish fears about the reputation for the honesty of Jewish businessmen are in part well-grounded. Blacks reacted negatively to the statement, but they were not nearly as negative as Jews expected. They disagreed by a relatively mild 44-36 percent.

On the negative-stereotype items, the results were as follows.

Although there was substantial agreement with the negative statements by blacks, in seven out of the ten items Jews believed blacks would be more negative and hostile than turned out to be the case. With non-Jewish whites, the estimates of anti-Jewish feeling by the Jews themselves were higher in ten out of the ten items. However, there is no doubt that Jews believed other groups in the population held negative views on Jews much more than these groups said they did.

Specifically, on the statement, "Jews are to ambitious for their own good," Jews expected blacks to agree by 54-24 percent. Blacks did agree, but by the narrow margin of 39-37 percent, or 15 percentage points below the Jewish estimate. Jews also expected non-Jewish whites to agree that Jews are over-ambitious by a slim 40-38 percent. Non-Jewish whites disagreed by an overwhelming 72-11 percent.

On the statement, "Jews are richer than other people," Jews expected blacks to agree by 78-13 percent. Blacks did agree, but by a lesser 69-16 percent. In the case of non-Jewish whites, Jews expected them to agree to the statement by 53-31 percent. In fact, non-Jewish whites disagreed with it by 44-36 percent.

Jews showed a high degree of negative expectation over the statement, "Most slum lords are Jewish." Among blacks, the Jewish estimate was that there would be an 80-9 percent division. Jews were not far off: blacks agreed by 73-8 percent. Jews also expected that non-Jewish whites would agree with the statement by 55-27 percent. A plurality of non-Jewish whites did agree, but by a much smaller 34-21 percent, with 45 percent unable to make any estimate. Puerto Ricans tended to agree with the statement by 50-12 percent.

Again, Jews overestimated the negative views of both groups in the case of the statement, "Jews stick to their own and never give an outsider a break." The Jews guessed that blacks would divide 54-25 in agreement. Blacks did agree, but by a lesser 49-31 percent, 5 percentage points below the Jewish estimate. Non-Jewish whites did disagree, but by a much more decisive 67-20 percent, 15 percentage points lower in the "agree" column.

The same pattern is evident in regard to the statement, "Jews feel superior to other groups." Jews expected blacks to agree with it by 57-22 percent. They were almost precisely correct on this score, with blacks agreeing by 53-22 percent, still 4 percentage points lower than Jewish estimates. Jews expected non-Jewish whites to agree by 40-38 percent. In fact, they disagreed by 50-27 percent, a gap of 13 percentage points.

A similar pattern appears on the statement, "Jewish businessmen will try to put over a shady deal on you." Jews expected that blacks would agree by a substantial 66-15 percent. Blacks did agree, but to a slightly lesser extent: 62-17 percent. Jews also expected non-Jewish whites to deny the statement 41-40 percent. They denied it by a substantial 66-17 percent.

The pattern shifts, however, over the statement, "Between money and people, Jews will choose money." Jews expected blacks to agree with the claim by 59-20 percent. In fact, blacks agreed with it by an overwhelming 71-11 percent. Jews also believed that non-Jewish whites would agree by a narrow 40-37 percent. But that group disagreed by 51-23 percent.

On another statement, "Jews are more a race than a religion," black reactions were underestimated and non-Jewish white overestimated by the Jews themselves. Jews expected blacks to agree with the claim by 54-24 percent. Blacks agreed by an even higher 57-26 percent. Jews also expected non-Jewish whites to agree by 44-34 percent, but they disagreed by a clear 53-32 percent.

On the statement, "Jews are more loyal to Israel than to America," Jewish expectations were that blacks would agree by 37-29 percent. Blacks did agree with that, but by a much higher 52-21 percent, or 15 percentage points above the Jewish estimate. On the other hand, Jews expected non-Jewish whites to disagree with the statement by 44-28 percent. They did disagree, but by a much higher 57-18 percent.

HOW JEWS ARE PERCEIVED

One clearly discernible pattern throughout is that, with only a few exceptions, the Jewish community tended to underestimate black belief in the favorable statements about them and also to overestimate most of the unfavorable stereotypes. With the non-Jewish white community, Jews tended to overestimate how that group feels about the positive stereotypes. However, at the same time Jews consistently overestimated the hostility of the non-Jewish whites in New York City.

Certainly, a generalized conclusion can be drawn that Jews tended to believe anti-Jewish feeling is worse than it is in reality and that their positive attributes are not as recognized as they are.

The claim is certain to be made that in answering stereotype questions such as these, most people are likely to overstate the positive and to understate their true feelings on the negative. However, by including in the analysis Jewish estimates for both the blacks and non-Jewish whites, a kind of control can be exercised on how much over/understating was taking place. It should be pointed out that the Jewish group underestimated black attitudes on three negative items and in all ten positive items. Jews also overestimated non-Jewish white attitudes on the positive side four times out of ten.

When the facts are looked at in terms of comparative black and non-Jewish totals, there are some clear patterns. There is no doubt that blacks were consistently more prone to hold to anti-Jewish stereotypes than non-Jewish whites. This is true in ten out of ten items, and the margins of difference are substantial. There is little doubt, then, that blacks were more likely to believe negatives about Jews than any other group.

But in the case of the positive attributes, blacks believed them in higher percentages than non-Jewish whites in five items and in lower percentages in five. Blacks tended to be far more generous toward Jews than Puerto Ricans were, but also more critical.

Blacks saw Jews as having mixed characteristics. Obviously, they were critical of Jews in the money area, and they also suspected that Jews control more of their economic life than other groups. But they also saw Jews as generous and as an oppressed minority.

It might be said that blacks showed themselves to be ambivalent and even uncertain in their views about Jews. Unquestionably they show some hostility. But to say that they were downright hostile would be to look only at the negative side of the scale. More likely, the answer to where blacks will end up in their stance toward Jews in New York is in the balance, depending on whether the positives are capitalized on. This, in turn, will depend on the efforts among both groups to close apparent gaps in perceptions and understanding.

WHAT BLACKS AND NON-JEWISH WHITES SAY ABOUT JEWS

Blacks and non-Jewish whites were both asked to put into their own words just what they like and don't like about Jews. On the positive side, the blacks tended to stress the success which Jews have had in getting ahead, their self-sacrifice and

TABLE 91

LIKES ABOUT JEWS: BLACKS

	Total Blacks [a] %
They stick together, support each other	13
Provide jobs, give you chance to prove yourself	8
Ambitious, better themselves, get educations	6
Successful in business and money, economic power	6
Considerate, kind, generous, try to help	5
Help blacks, give blacks a break	4
Educate children, effective parents, children succeed	4
Progressive, liberal	2
Thrifty, careful, save money	2
They study and work hard	2
They are fair, not prejudiced	2
They are aggressive	2
Very religious	2
Support the underdog, civil liberties	2
Friendly	2
Can't generalize	21
Like nothing whatsoever about Jews	12
Not sure	19

[a] Adds to more than 100 percent as some respondents volunteered more than one answer.

hard work, their willingness to give blacks a break. In almost all cases, the blacks tended to view the Jews as potential employers or people one had to do business with, or as tough, disciplined people who had made it the hard way, but who could be generous, too.

An 81-year-old black in Brooklyn's Bedford-Stuyvesant Section who lives on his social security allotment put it this way: "Give them credit for being so aggressive in getting ahead in the business world. Nobody would give them a break at all. So, naturally, they take care of their own kind." A 59-year-old black clerical worker in Manhattan, earning $5,500 a year, said, "They treat you better than your black neighbor

TABLE 92

DISLIKES ABOUT JEWS: BLACKS

	Total Blacks [a] %
Too interested in money, greedy	8
Cheat, unethical, ruthless, take advantage in business	7
As employers: demanding, pay little, use you	7
Slumlords (stores and apartments), take money out of area	6
Think they are better, arrogant	5
Cheap, tight, stingy	5
Aggressive, pushy	4
Clannish, try to keep power for themselves	4
Prejudiced, keep other minorities down	4
Too rich, powerful	2
They don't understand blacks	1
A whitey is a whitey	1
No contact with Jews	1
Just don't like them	3
Can't generalize	31
Not sure	20

[a] Adds to more than 100 percent as some respondents volunteered more than one answer.

in business if you work for them." A black maintenance worker in the garment district, earning $4,200 a year, added, "They will give the black man work. They will even give you an opportunity to advance once in a while." A black office manager in Harlem who earns $13,000 a year spoke with admiration for Jewish people: "They're independent, they help each other. Why, they are the wealthiest people on earth."

A statistical summary of the things blacks said they liked about Jews is shown in Table 91.

Dislike of Jews among blacks centers mainly on money, the claim that Jews are "too greedy," "ruthless and cheating," "as employers always demanding from you," "as slumlords taking money out of the area," "cheap and stingy." A 28-year-old store clerk in Queens put it this way, "Money is their God. They don't care how it is made or who gets hurt. Money is what counts, man." A 30-year-old black mother on welfare added, "They own most of the tenements in Harlem and they allow us to have a roof over our heads, but that roof leaks all the time and we pay through the nose to have it." A 22-year-old technician in Manhattan, earning $5,200 a year, said, "They work you too hard. They watch you constantly or have their families watch for them." A 28-year-old unskilled laborer in the South Bronx, earning $6,200 annually, added, "I just don't trust any of them. They will swindle you and try to work you to death."

A summary of black dislikes of Jews in New York City is shown in Table 92.

Non-Jewish whites tended to think far more in personalized terms about Jews. They think of Jews as "friendly, pleasant, nice," "people with strong family ties," "considerate, kind, generous," "industrious, want to better themselves," as well as "successful." A 21-year-old Italian service worker in Queens, earning $8,000, put it this way, "They are friendly. And they always want to educate their children and work hard to get ahead. You can't knock that." An actress and producer in Manhattan who is a white Protestant, earning $13,000 a year, said, "I've lived with them most of my life. They are such warm human beings." A professional man with the telephone company, who is Catholic, earns $25,000 a year and lives in Queens, ticked off these items of praise for Jewish people: "They know culture and believe in education. They have family warmth and solidarity. They have a social consciousness. They are generous with charity work. They're great." In Brooklyn, a Catholic engineer earning $18,500 added, "They are very concerned about their children. Like the Catholics, they know the family is most important."

HOW JEWS ARE PERCEIVED

Table 93 summarizes how all of the positive, "like," comments about Jews added up among non-Jewish whites.

TABLE 93

LIKES ABOUT JEWS: NON-JEWISH WHITES

	Total Non-Jewish Whites %
They are friendly, pleasant, nice people	14
Strong family ties, educate their children	11
Considerate, kind, generous	11
Study, work hard, industrious	8
They stick together, back each other up	7
Are ambitious to better themselves	7
Successful in money matters	6
Smart, intelligent	4
Good, fair employers	4
Value scholarship	4
Give to charities	2
Mind their own business	2
Will give you chance to prove yourself	2
Support underdog	1
Are proud, won't beg	1
Thrifty, save money	1
Progressive, liberal	1
Can't generalize	22
Like nothing about them	3
Not sure	9

Volunteered responses on dislikes about Jews among non-Jewish whites were relatively few. But they, too, centered on personal characteristics perceived in Jews--"clannish," "arrogant, think they are better than others," "aggressive and pushy." A service worker of English descent in Brooklyn said, "They push so hard. They are very shrewd. They want to be in control over everything they touch." A 52-year-old financial clerk of Irish descent in Staten Island said, "They

TABLE 94

DISLIKES ABOUT JEWS: NON-JEWISH WHITES

	Total Non-Jewish Whites %
Too clannish	6
Arrogant, think they are better than others	5
Aggressive, pushy	5
Unethical in business	4
Greedy, just out for money	3
Cheap, tight, stingy	2
Discourteous, bad manners, loud	2
Demanding employers	1
Nothing against them	53
Not sure	19

are all out for the Jews, period. And they are so loud-mouthed about it." A Greek headwaiter in Manhattan said, "They just like to stick their noses into things all the time and it's none of their business, you know."

A summary of the volunteered comments on the negative side about Jews by non-Jewish whites is shown in Table 94.

It is apparent from the comments of the non-Jewish whites that for the most part they felt confident enough to look on the Jews as one of a number of groups of people who make up the polyglot that is New York.

By contrast, those blacks who could generalize about Jews (31 percent said they could not generalize) talked about Jews in terms of how they might affect the blacks' own daily lives as employers, as government employees, as owners of stores and tenements--in short, as an integral part of the power establishment which has not treated them especially well.

JEWS ESTIMATE ANTI-SEMITISM

The Jewish cross-section was asked to estimate the amount of anti-semitism which exists among key groups and institutions

HOW JEWS ARE PERCEIVED

in the non-Jewish community. A summary of these estimates is shown in Table 95.

The range of perceived anti-Semitism was extensive, with black militants at the top of the list (68 percent "a lot") and people of Italian descent, policemen, and apartment real estate agents at the bottom (all 3 percent "a lot"). Out of the top five on the list, three were drawn from the ranks of blacks: black militants (68 percent), black teenagers (42 percent), and black adults (32 percent). The other two are interesting: "right-wingers like the John Birchers" (59 percent "a lot") and "private clubs" (35 percent "a lot"). These two, of course are white, one politically threatening and the other representative of an establishment which the Jews tend to feel excludes them socially (as indeed it often does).

This felt anti-Semitism on the part of the mainstream white establishment cuts quite deep among Jewish people in New York City. White Anglo-Saxon Protestants were thought to be anti-Semitic "some" to "a lot" by 54 percent of the Jews, compared with 41 percent who felt that Catholics are just as prejudiced against them. Next come "men who own big corporations," thought to be at least "some" to "a lot" anti-Semitic by 56 percent of the Jewish group.

In the line-up of white ethnic groups, Jews tended to see people of German descent as more anti-Semitic than those of Irish descent, although Italians were seen as least against the Jews. An exception to the greater suspicion of Protestants than of Catholics, however, emerges in the case of white Protestant ministers, who were felt to be less prejudiced than Catholic priests.

The sense among Jews that right-wingers and members of the WASP establishment are anti-Semitic, of course, has existed for many years. But as of mid-1969, it could be said that the blacks had supplanted these more traditional enemies.

Of course, perception of which people and groups are anti-Semitic is relative even within the Jewish community. The divisions among Jews on just how anti-Semitic black adults are (shown in Table 96) run according to the pattern already familiar in responses to other questions in this study.

The breakdown borough shows that a majority of Brooklyn Jews felt that a majority of black adults are anti-Semitic, compared with only 16 percent of the Jews in Queens and Manhattan. Conservative Jews tended to feel this way slightly more than Orthodox Jews, but both felt this way more than did Reform Jews and substantially more than did non-affiliated Jews. Those Jews over 50 felt that black adults are more anti-Semitic than

TABLE 95

JEWISH PERCEPTIONS OF
EXTENT OF ANTI-SEMITISM BY KEY GROUPS

	A Lot %	Some, Not A Lot %	Almost None %	Not Sure %
Anti-Semitism Among:				
Black militants	68	17	4	11
Right-wingers like John Birchers	59	16	6	19
Black teenagers	42	32	9	17
Private clubs	35	36	12	17
Black adults	32	41	12	15
White Anglo-Saxon Protestants	22	32	21	25
Men who own big corporations	18	38	25	19
People of German descent	14	33	27	26
Medical schools	12	33	37	18
White Catholic priests	7	30	34	29
Catholics	7	34	30	29
Building trades unions	6	20	33	41
People of Irish descent	5	30	34	31
White Protestant ministers	4	26	41	29
Policemen	3	22	55	20
Apartment real estate agents	3	28	51	18
People of Italian descent	3	23	49	25

TABLE 96

JEWISH ESTIMATIONS OF ANTI-SEMITISM IN BLACK ADULTS

	A Lot %	Some, Not A Lot %	Almost None %	Not Sure %
Total Jewish	32	41	12	15
Manhattan	16	46	11	27
Bronx	27	47	17	9
Queens	16	55	15	14
Brooklyn	54	23	7	16
Orthodox	39	42	8	11
Conservative	41	35	10	14
Reform	34	36	15	15
Non-affiliated	14	51	15	20
21 - 34	28	38	15	19
35 - 49	27	50	8	15
Over 50	37	38	11	14
Under $10,000	43	31	11	15
$10,000-$15,000	21	49	13	17
Over $15,000	25	48	11	16
8th grade	48	31	8	13
High school	34	40	10	16
College	25	44	14	17

young Jews did. Those with incomes under $10,000 felt it much more strongly than those above $10,000, and those with less than a high school education felt it much more than those with college training. These differences are substantial and significant. They show the dominant split in the Jewish community.

However, this pattern does not hold for a more esoteric form of anti-Semitism, one which is more likely to affect the upper reaches of Jewish society in Manhattan, the higher income and better-educated segments of the Jewish community--anti-Semitism by private clubs. Jewish estimates of the extent of anti-Semitism by such Clubs are summarized in Table 97.

The breakdown by age, education, and other factors shows that the pattern has shifted. By borough, more Jews who live in Manhattan and in Queens felt there is "a lot" of anti-Semitism by private clubs than was the case among Jews in the Bronx or Brooklyn. Orthodox Jews felt least strongly about this form of anti-Semitism. Young people under 35 years of age felt as strongly about it as those over 50. The group with annual incomes of over $15,000 believed there is more anti-Semitism from private clubs than did those whose incomes are under $10,000. The college-educated segment felt it more than the segment with an eighth grade education.

Clearly, anti-semitism is a relative matter. More privileged Jews feel it when they come up against the essentially white Protestant corporate world of New York, which is the establishment not only in the city but for much of the nation and the world. This world does not immediately affect Jews in the outlying boroughs of Brooklyn and the Bronx, who make their livings and pass most of their lives outside of the mainstream of Manhattan. To them, the blacks, however, are real and part of their daily lives, whether they are moving into their neighborhoods in the Bronx or trying to change the school system in Ocean Hill-Brownsville.

The Jewish group was asked to estimate how many non-Jewish whites and how many blacks were anti-Semitic; the responses to this question are summarized in Table 98.

The breakdown of estimates on the extent of anti-Semitism among blacks shows a pattern again sharply dividing the Jewish community (see Table 99).

The borough-by-borough breakdown showed a difference once again. Manhattan and Queens Jews were least willing to say that "most blacks are anti-Semitic," while Brooklyn Jews felt that "most blacks are anti-Semitic" most, by a wide margin. Orthodox Jews were much more prepared to make the charge, as were older Jews and as were those Jews who had the least education. The young, the best-educated segment, the non-affiliated, and the Reform Jews lined up on the other side, as least prepared to make the charge.

The Jewish community was asked whether the blacks or the non-Jewish whites are a greater threat today to the Jews. Responses to this question are shown in Table 100.

Significantly, a majority of Jewish people in New York City could make a choice between the two groups. Thirty percent singled out the blacks, 22 percent the non-Jewish whites, and another 15 percent said "both groups." Only 12 percent said "neither," and 21 percent were uncertain.

TABLE 97

JEWISH PERCEPTIONS OF EXTENT OF ANTI-SEMITISM BY PRIVATE CLUBS

	A Lot %	Some, Not A Lot %	Almost None %	Not Sure %
Total Jewish	35	36	12	17
Manhattan	39	41	6	14
Bronx	31	34	18	17
Queens	41	46	6	7
Brooklyn	33	26	15	26
Orthodox	30	34	8	28
Conservative	38	33	12	17
Reform	34	38	15	13
Non-affiliated	38	39	13	10
21 - 34	34	40	11	15
35 - 49	38	42	6	14
Over 50	34	30	16	20
Under $10,000	35	32	13	20
$10,000 - $15,000	31	42	12	15
Over $15,000	37	39	10	14
8th grade	28	31	13	28
High school	39	35	12	14
College	34	39	11	16

TABLE 98

JEWISH PERCEPTIONS OF EXTENT OF ANTI-SEMITISM AMONG NON-JEWISH WHITES AND BLACKS

	Non-Jewish Whites %	Blacks %
Most	9	23
Some, not a lot	63	57
Hardly any	16	11
Not sure	12	9

TABLE 99

JEWISH PERCEPTIONS OF EXTENT OF ANTI-SEMITISM AMONG BLACKS OF ALL AGES

	Most %	Some, Not A Lot %	Hardly Any %	Not Sure %
Total Jewish	23	57	11	9
Manhattan	14	59	13	14
Bronx	22	65	9	4
Queens	14	64	14	8
Brooklyn	34	47	9	10
Orthodox	38	47	8	7
Conservative	27	55	8	10
Reform	20	53	14	13
Non-affiliated	7	73	14	6
21 - 34	17	62	13	8
35 - 49	18	60	10	12
50 and over	31	51	10	8
8th grade	40	46	7	7
High school	26	53	10	11
College	14	64	13	9

In a straight-out division between the blacks and non-Jewish whites, Jews in Brooklyn, by better than 2 to 1, selected the blacks as the greater threat. Bronx Jews were evenly split down the middle. Queens and Manhattan Jews tended by narrow margins to say that non-Jewish whites are more of a threat.

However, among all three of the divisions of the Jewish faith, a plurality picked the blacks over the other whites as the greatest threat. The Jews picking the non-Jewish whites were those who do not identify themselves with a particular wing of Judiasm. The young tended to name whites as a greater threat, as is the case among the college-educated, segment. The older and less well educated Jews veered heavily over to the blacks as the real threat.

HOW JEWS ARE PERCEIVED

TABLE 100

JEWISH PERCEPTIONS OF BLACKS OR NON-JEWISH WHITES AS GREATER THREAT TO JEWS

	Blacks %	Non-Jewish Whites %	Neither[a] %	Both[a] %	Not Sure %
Total Jewish	30	22	12	15	21
Manhattan	19	20	11	17	33
Bronx	29	29	12	15	15
Queens	24	27	19	8	22
Brooklyn	39	16	8	18	19
Orthodox	36	11	11	23	19
Conservative	43	18	8	13	18
Reform	26	17	16	18	23
Non-affiliated	15	43	12	6	24
21-34	20	30	15	10	25
35-49	33	19	13	17	18
50 and over	37	16	10	18	19
8th grade	45	11	6	18	20
High school	33	18	10	16	23
College	23	28	16	13	20

Suspicion of blacks lies deep in some segments of Jewish society in New York today, as this study of attitudes has repeatedly shown. The center of the feeling is in Brooklyn, among Orthodox Jews, among the less educated, less affluent, and older people.

This part of the Jewish community is still a minority, almost balanced off by Manhattan, Queens, non-affiliated, younger, more affluent, more educated Jews who identify less with a particular segment of their religion.

The balance in the center of the Jewish community is made up of the Bronx Jews, Reform Jews, and those between 35 and 49. In the study they were consistently between the polar groups--in concern about the black threat in the city, in their perception of discrimination against blacks, and in their feeling of being threatened by blacks.

In its perception of blacks, the Jewish community is clearly not monolithic. However, the traditional reputation of Jewish support of the underdog, no matter what his color, creed, race, or national origin, has been shaken to the core among some segments of the community.

CHAPTER 5 — THE TRIGGER OF POLARIZATION: THE NEW YORK CITY SCHOOL DISPUTE

In the history of attitudes of races toward each other, it is not often that any single event or series of events can be singled out as a central cause or even as a starting point of a change. But in the case of Jewish-black attitudes toward each other in New York City, there is little doubt that the events of 1967 and 1968 which culminated in three teacher strikes marked a decisive turning point.

The events themselves have been treated elsewhere--occasionally with dispassion but more frequently in passionate tracts representing the teachers', the local governing board's, the Jewish, the black or the Board of Education's point of view. As was reported earlier, blacks, Jews, and non-Jewish whites all are agreed on one central fact: the school dispute was a single, pinpointed, and massive episode that changed Jewish-black relations in New York City.

From the teachers' union standpoint, the dispute itself centered on the right of teachers to job security and protection from physical manhandling in the performance of their duties in black and Puerto Rican experimental school districts run by local governing boards. From the black standpoint, the dispute stemmed from the refusal of the white establishment to allow blacks the right to determine the conditions under which their children were to be educated. The central characters in the drama were Albert Shanker, the Jewish president of the United Federation of Teachers, Rhody McCoy, the black head of the Ocean Hill-Brownsville experimental school district; the New York City Board of Education; the New York State Education Commissioner, James Allen; and the Mayor of the city of New York, John Lindsay. Most of the teachers were Jewish, while most of McCoy's constituents in Ocean Hill-Brownsville were black.

TABLE 101

SIDE PERCEIVED AS MORE RIGHT IN TEACHER STRIKE: CITY-WIDE

	Teachers' Union %	Local Governing Board %	Neither[a] %	Both[a] %	Not Sure %
Total City	40	18	12	6	24
Jewish	63	8	10	5	14
Black	14	50	10	6	20
White Catholic	48	9	14	3	26
Puerto Rican	21	12	11	8	48
White Protestant	35	20	18	9	18
Manhattan	22	28	12	8	30
Bronx	47	14	14	4	21
Queens	46	15	12	7	20
Brooklyn	47	16	12	3	22
Richmond	82	--	6	6	6

[a] Volunteered response.

Irrespective of the merits of the dispute, the whole episode divided New York City as it has rarely been divided before. Viewed in mid-1969 after the dispute seemed ended, if not entirely settled, the teachers' union was ahead. There were many, though, who thought neither side had won, that both had won, or were not sure. There was divided opinion too, on which side had been more right. Table 101 summarizes city opinion on this issue.

City-wide, the teachers' union was viewed as being right by 40 percent, the local governing board by 18 percent, neither by 12 percent, both by 6 percent, and nearly one in four--24 percent--simply had no final judgment.

But the over-all results hardly begin to tell the real story. Most solidly behind the teachers was the Jewish group: 63 percent pro-union and only 8 percent for the governing board. Most solidly behind the governing board was the black group, by 50-14 percent.

The second most sizable bloc of support for the teachers' union can be found among the white Catholics, who sided with

TABLE 102

SIDE PERCEIVED AS MORE RIGHT IN TEACHER STRIKE: BLACKS

	Teachers' Union %	Local Governing Board %	Neither[a] %	Both[a] %	Not Sure %
Total Blacks	14	50	10	6	20
Manhattan	14	50	11	7	18
Bronx	24	41	7	5	23
Queens	10	62	12	7	9
Brooklyn	12	48	10	5	25
8th grade	19	39	8	7	27
High school	13	51	11	5	20
College	12	59	12	7	10
Under $3,000	19	38	11	7	25
$3,000-$6,999	15	49	9	4	23
$7,000+	11	57	13	8	11

[a] Volunteered response.

them by a lopsided 48-9 percent. White Protestants tended not to be drawn into support for either (45 percent would not name either group as being right), but by 35-20 percent were more on the side of the teachers. The Puerto Ricans were most reluctant to take sides, two out of every three refusing to state a categorical sympathy for either the teachers' union or the local governing board. However, among those who would, the teachers' union was supported by 21-12 percent.

The results, therefore, point to the fact that in crude terms the school dispute left the black community isolated as the only group with even plurality sympathies for the local governing board. Clearly, Jewish attitudes were at the opposite pole. But the Jews were able to find a sizable part of all other communities more on the teachers' than on the governing board's side.

It is significant to point out that 29 percent of the Jewish and 36 percent of the black people did not choose sides. This reinforces the point that all Jews are not against all blacks or vice versa.

The results by borough are revealing. Only in Manhattan did a bare 28-22 percent plurality back the governing board. The Bronx, Queens, and Brooklyn all divided roughly three to one on the side of the teachers' union. Staten Island, almost all white, easily the most Catholic, the least Jewish, and the most conservative of the boroughs, recorded 82 percent on the side of the union, and none backing the local governing board.

There were sharp divisions within the black community, as Table 102 shows. Affluence within the black group provides a real key: the higher-income and the better-educated blacks were decidedly behind the local governing board and less in support of the teachers' union.

It is significant that the most privileged blacks were most solidly behind the local governing board. It is this same group which most rejected the goal of "tearing down white society."

Within the Jewish community, the lines of division closely parallel basic racial attitudes, as the breakdown by borough, religious affiliation, age, and education in Table 103 shows.

Leading the way in support of the teachers' union were Jews in Brooklyn and the Bronx, Orthodox Jews, those over 50, and those with a high school education (just ahead of those who had not been to high school). Table 104 shows the division among all three key groups by age and education.

As has already been pointed out, Jews as a whole showed more support for the teachers' union than other groups in the city, and blacks more support for the local governing board. Jews under 35 and those with a college education tended to be more sympathetic to the local governing board than older, less well educated Jews, though even in these groups substantial majorities said the teachers' union was more right in the strike.

Among non-Jewish whites, who came out for the teachers over the local board by considerably smaller margins than the Jews, the young and the college educated also gave more support to the local governing board than did other segments.

In the black group the young, the middle-aged, and the college educated gave the strongest support to the local governing board.

The data show that all groups of Jews were more on the teachers' side than other groups in the city. However, with the exception of the change in position of eighth-grade and high school educated groups, the pattern of support for the teachers' union directly reflects Jewish attitudes toward blacks. While it might be argued that these pro-union groups were made

TABLE 103

SIDE PERCEIVED AS MORE RIGHT IN TEACHER STRIKE: JEWS

	Teachers' Union %	Local Governing Board %	Neither[a] %	Both[a] %	Not Sure %
Total Jewish	63	8	10	5	14
Manhattan	41	14	10	9	26
Bronx	71	5	9	5	10
Queens	60	9	11	6	14
Brooklyn	72	5	9	2	12
Orthodox	79	1	5	2	13
Conservative	73	1	7	5	14
Reform	65	5	9	5	16
Non-affiliated	36	24	19	8	13
21-34	56	13	8	8	15
35-49	60	11	9	4	16
50+	69	2	11	3	15
8th grade	69	4	7	2	18
High school	71	4	7	2	16
College	53	12	13	8	14

[a] Volunteered response.

hostile to blacks in New York City by the school dispute, it is also possible that the school dispute brought to the surface in the Jewish community a latent pattern of attitudes toward blacks that may well be difficult to change.

Both the Irish and the Italian Catholics were more on the side of the union than were either white Catholics as a whole or non-Jewish whites who belong to a union (see Table 105).

The substantial difference between white Catholic union members and the Italian and Irish groups indicates clearly that something more than simply being for or against trade unions was at stake in the school dispute. For it would have been likely that the white union members would have been among the staunchest backers of fellow unionists on strike. That this

TABLE 104

SIDE PERCEIVED AS MORE RIGHT IN TEACHER STRIKE: BY AGE AND EDUCATION

	Teachers' Union %	Local Governing Board %	Neither[a] %	Both[a] %	Not Sure %
Total Jewish	<u>63</u>	<u>8</u>	<u>10</u>	<u>5</u>	<u>14</u>
21-34	56	13	8	8	15
35-49	60	11	9	4	16
50+	69	2	11	3	15
8th grade	69	4	7	2	18
High School	71	4	7	2	16
College	53	12	13	8	14
Total Blacks	<u>14</u>	<u>50</u>	<u>10</u>	<u>6</u>	<u>20</u>
21-34	16	53	8	6	17
35-49	12	53	13	5	17
50+	16	37	11	8	28
8th grade	19	39	8	7	27
High school	13	51	11	5	20
College	12	59	12	7	10
Total Non-Jewish Whites	<u>38</u>	<u>12</u>	<u>14</u>	<u>6</u>	<u>30</u>
21-34	37	18	11	5	29
35-49	42	7	15	6	30
50+	35	9	17	8	31
No college	37	9	14	5	35
Some college	41	22	12	7	18

[a] Volunteered response.

THE NEW YORK CITY SCHOOL DISPUTE 137

TABLE 105

SIDE PERCEIVED AS MORE RIGHT IN TEACHER
STRIKE: WHITE CATHOLICS AND NON-JEWISH
WHITE UNION MEMBERS

	Teachers' Union %	Local Governing Board %	Neither[a] %	Both[a] %	Not Sure %
Total White Catholics	48	9	14	3	26
Italian	51	5	15	3	26
Irish	57	4	13	2	24
Total Non-Jewish Whites Who belong to union	41	11	14	5	29

[a] Volunteered response.

was not the case indicates the importance of the issues not related to union rights in the dispute.

Both blacks and Jews were asked to state in their own words what were the real issues behind the teacher strike. Blacks tended to see the issue in terms of black community control of the schools. An unemployed 29-year-old woman in Harlem put it this way: "Shanker wants to see blacks without power. Ocean Hill wanted a better education for blacks. This caused a power struggle." A black 21-year-old laborer in Queens said: "I think it is the people's right to decide about the quality of their children's education. The teachers and their job security was a hoax. The union leadership was against blacks and decentralization since it started." A 58-year-old black foreman in Harlem, earning $13,000 a year, added: "As I see it, we want our children to get a better education. The local boards want to make sure that the teachers are qualified--white or black." A 25-year-old black laborer in Brooklyn's Bedford-Stuyvesant section, earning $4,700 a year, said: "The governing board wants good teachers for black and Puerto Rican children, not someone to tell them to drop dead."

Table 106 shows the results when all the black volunteered comments are added up.

TABLE 106

PERCEPTION OF REAL ISSUES IN TEACHERS' STRIKE: BLACKS

	Total Blacks %
Power struggle for control of schools	14
Parents wanted more voice in child's education	13
Job security, protection of teachers' jobs	10
Teachers wanted more money, benefits	9
Parents wanted better education and teachers	9
Racial issue, discrimination	6
Whether decentralization would reduce power of union	6
Teachers' union is anti-black	5
Teachers resisting being accountable to parents	4
Blacks not wanting whites running black schools	3
Jews wanted to retain control	2
Economic issue	2
Not sure	17

The Jewish community tended to see the basic issue in the teacher strikes as job security for the teachers. A 42-year-old skilled craftsman in Brooklyn put it this way: "The governing board wanted control. The teachers were afraid of their jobs if the board got control." A Jewish business executive in Manhattan said: "Job security was the name of the game. The parents wanted to establish their right to override teacher job security. Someone had to lose. In the end, the Jews had the power and won." A 63-year-old Jewish social worker in Brooklyn said: "Tenure for teachers was at stake. This was the only way the whole system could be preserved. Otherwise it would have been anarchy." A Brooklyn Jewish businessman earning over $20,000 a year put it this way: "I feel the local Ocean Hill-Brownsville governing board was way out of line, usurping power beyond any reasonable limit. They wanted the power of management to destroy teacher rights. Teacher rights had to win."

Table 107 shows the results when all the Jewish answers are put in statistical terms.

TABLE 107

PERCEPTION OF REAL ISSUES IN
TEACHERS' STRIKE: JEWS

	Total Jewish %
Justice and job security for teachers	24
Blacks wanted to push everyone else around	9
Local governing board vs. union	8
Black prejudice against whites	8
Desire for black teachers in schools	7
Power struggle between blacks and whites	5
Teachers were threatened, abused	5
Blacks tried to get rid of teachers	4
Money, economic issue	4
Blacks trying to break union	4
Excessives on both sides	4
Dispute over decentralization	3
Parent vs. professional control of curriculum	3
Teachers wanted disruptive kids out	2
Selection of teachers and control of budget	2
Anti-Semitism	2
Community trying to put in unqualified teachers	2
Not sure	14

Thus, blacks tended to put their conception of the school dispute in terms of the rights of parents, with less emphasis on racial differences. But among Jews, the central issue of job security was closely followed by complaints about blacks being "too pushy," about "black prejudice against whites," "power struggle between blacks and whites," "blacks trying to get rid of teachers," "blacks trying to break the union," "blacks threatening teachers." There were more volunteered comments among the Jewish group about "black" activity than there were parallel "Jewish" overtones among the blacks.

At the heart of the substance of the dispute was the future of community influence in running the schools. The total cross-section of city opinion was asked how it felt about the community's current influence; results were as shown in Table 108.

TABLE 108

ATTITUDE TOWARD COMMUNITY INFLUENCE
IN RUNNING SCHOOLS IN THIS NEIGHBORHOOD:
CITY-WIDE

	Too Much %	Too Little %	Right Amount %	Not Sure %
Total City	8	29	23	40
Jewish	10	20	27	43
Black	11	56	12	21
White Catholic	6	21	24	49
Puerto Rican	7	24	24	45
White Protestant	7	25	27	41

The striking part of the answers on community influence in the schools is that even after the controversy which divided New York City, 40 percent of the adult population were not able to make up their minds. Among the remaining 60 percent with opinions, the division was close, with 31 percent opposed to more community influence and 29 percent favoring more.

The blacks stand out as easily the most decided group on the community influence issue and the most committed to increasing community influence in the schools. Eight in ten of them had opinions, and 56 percent were clearly on the side of wanting more influence for the local community. Jews showed far less certainty on the issue, although by almost two to one those with opinions tended to be for maintaining the status quo rather than increasing community control. White Catholics and Puerto Ricans registered as three to two against more community influence.

Table 109 shows division by age and education within the three key groups.

There are sharp differences within the black community. Younger blacks and the better educated clearly felt most strongly about community influence. Not only were they involved as parents with their children's education, but they were also likely to be most articulate in stating their demands.

Among Jews, the younger and the college-educated groups were more apt to say there is too little, rather than too much,

TABLE 109

ATTITUDE TOWARD COMMUNITY INFLUENCE IN RUNNING SCHOOLS IN THIS NEIGHBORHOOD: BY AGE AND EDUCATION

	Too Much %	Too Little %	Right Amount %	Not Sure %
Total Jewish	10	20	27	43
21-34	6	25	28	41
35-49	10	27	35	28
50 and over	14	12	22	52
8th grade	15	7	14	64
High school	14	16	24	46
College	6	27	33	34
Total Blacks	11	56	12	21
21-34	10	64	7	19
35-49	11	57	15	17
50 and over	15	37	19	29
8th grade	19	43	11	27
High school	11	58	12	19
College	6	64	13	17
Total Non-Jewish White	6	25	24	45
21-34	8	29	20	43
35-49	3	22	34	41
50 and over	8	21	18	53
No college	6	21	25	48
Some college	8	35	22	35

community influence; the same holds true among non-Jewish whites.

The total city-wide cross-section was questioned on attitudes toward school decentralization. On this question the division was quite different, pro-decentralization emerging on top by a 35-25 percent margin, as Table 110 shows.

TABLE 110

ATTITUDE TOWARD SCHOOL DECENTRALIZATION:
CITY-WIDE

	Favor %	Oppose %	Depends[a] %	Not Sure %
Total City	35	25	10	30
Jewish	27	33	14	26
Black	61	12	8	19
White Catholic	27	31	8	34
Puerto Rican	21	20	14	45
White Protestant	36	29	7	28
Manhattan	41	17	11	31
Bronx	35	29	10	26
Queens	33	27	9	31
Brooklyn	30	29	11	30
Richmond	38	32	8	22

[a] Volunteered response.

Jews and white Catholics were against decentralization, but by only small margins. Puerto Ricans were split down the middle. White Protestants favored the concept. Blacks were overwhelmingly in favor of decentralization, by 61-12 percent. By borough, Manhattan was most for decentralization, but every borough recorded a plurality in support of it--even Brooklyn, albeit by 1 percentage point.

Table 111 shows the city-wide breakdown among key groups by age and education.

The young of all groups tended to favor decentralization more than their elders. The age difference is most marked

TABLE 111

ATTITUDE TOWARD SCHOOL DECENTRALIZATION:
BY AGE AND EDUCATION

	Favor %	Oppose %	Depends[a] %	Not Sure %
Total Jewish	27	33	14	26
21-34	38	29	13	20
35-49	27	41	12	20
50 and over	16	32	15	37
8th grade	9	29	13	49
High school	20	39	11	30
College	37	30	17	16
Total Blacks	61	12	8	19
21-34	64	10	7	19
35-49	64	11	8	17
50 and over	48	17	9	26
8th grade	54	12	8	26
High school	61	12	8	19
College	71	13	7	9
Total Non-Jewish White	29	26	9	36
21-34	33	27	8	32
35-49	27	25	11	37
50 and over	25	26	8	41
No college	23	26	10	41
Some college	48	25	6	21

[a] Volunteered response.

among Jews, in this group, those under 35 said they favored decentralization by a plurality of 38-29 percent.

There is a difference by education; the college educated of all groups were more in favor of decentralization than were the less educated. Among non-Jewish whites, for example, the group as a whole split 29-26 percent in favor; however, the college educated favored decentralization by the substantially larger plurality of 48-25 percent.

Earlier Harris surveys of public opinion in New York City conducted closer to the time of the events in the fall of 1968 showed decentralization as opposed by a 4 percent margin city-wide. The later results indicate that the basic concept of decentralization could be a relatively popular approach to education in the city, especially among blacks, and to a lesser extent among the college educated and the young of all groups. Clearly, the school dispute dampened enthusiasm for it. But even after all of the events which have scarred New York, the decentralization idea remains relatively well accepted with apparently growing support.

Blacks tended to see decentralization as a means to increase parental involvement and thus improve education. A black lab technician in the south Bronx put it this way: "Our schools are overcrowded and our children have not been able to get the attention they should. Decentralization would do away with problems of this kind."

A 21-year old black student in Queens said: "It is best for our children and theirs. This is a better understanding that has been held back for so long. Children were brainwashed before."

A 24-year-old unemployed black in the Ocean Hill-Brownsville area added: "Each area has its own problems. This decentralization would give the children a chance for more quality education."

A summary of black reasoning on school decentralization is shown in Table 112.

The Jewish group was divided on decentralization. Opposition centered around two concerns: "local boards are not qualified" and "education should be left to the professionals." A Jewish lawyer in Brooklyn, earning $25,000 a year, said: "The school system shouldn't be broken down and left in the hands of people who are not capable. It should be left to professional educators." A 67-year-old small confectionery store owner in Brooklyn added: "School ought to be run by people who are qualified, not just a bunch of loudmouths off the streets." Jews for decentralization pointed to the need

TABLE 112

FEELINGS BEHIND VIEWS ON SCHOOL DECENTRALIZATION: BLACKS

	Total Blacks[a] %
Why Favor:	**68**
Parents, community should have more voice	19
Parent participation will improve education	14
Blacks should control own schools as whites do	7
Schools need improvement, change	7
Parents know what is best for their children	6
Each community should handle its own problems	6
Community could get the teachers it wants	4
Increases sense of community involvement	3
Central boards don't consider, local, unique needs	2
Why Oppose:	**6**
Parents not qualified to run schools	3
Need central authority to get things done	2
Community not able to handle own problems	1
Depends on Who Is in Charge	**4**
Don't Know Anything About It	**8**
Not Sure	**20**

[a] Adds to more than 100 percent as some respondents volunteered more than one answer.

for local control. A doctor in Brooklyn said: "Local people, if carefully selected, will be the best judge of what is good for that community." A manager of a retail store in Brooklyn, earning $22,500 a year, put it this way: "The local community will get closer to the problem, if properly controlled. They can do nothing but good for the system." A Jewish social worker in Queens added: "The schools have been in a mess for so many years because of bigness and bureaucracy. Let the local community take over as they now do in the suburbs."

A statistical summary of Jewish reasoning on decentralization is shown in Table 113.

TABLE 113

FEELINGS BEHIND VIEWS ON DECENTRALIZATION: JEWS

	Total Jewish %
Why Favor:	**28**
Community should have say over education	8
Local people know their own needs	8
City too large for one board to handle	3
Schools not working well	3
Would bring peace	3
Other (favor)	3
Why Oppose:	**39**
Local boards not qualified	13
Leave to professionals	8
System fine the way it is	5
Local control too chaotic	3
Caused trouble	3
Some advocates looking for power	3
Would result in qualified whites being replaced by blacks unfairly	1
Other (oppose)	3
Can Work If Community Is Responsible	**6**
Community and Professionals Should Have Control	**5**
Not Sure	**26**

The margin of support for decentralization is not overwhelming. But it appears to be on the rise. The irony of the 1967-68 school dispute may well be that decentralization--the basic substantive issue in the controversy--will have won the day, but at the same time the racial cleavages it produced will have been exacerbated.

There have been claims that one of the deep-seated issues involved in the Ocean Hill-Brownsville dispute was a desire on the part of blacks to have their children taught by members of their own race. At best, only a minority of blacks said they feel this way (see Table 114).

TABLE 114

TEACHER PREFERENCE BY RACE: CITY-WIDE

	Prefer Black %	Prefer White %	No Difference %	Not Sure %
Total City	6	10	78	6
Jewish	1	11	83	5
Black	29	2	66	3
White Catholic	1	15	77	7
Puerto Rican	1	7	83	9
White Protestant	--	7	88	5

TABLE 115

TEACHER PREFERENCE BY RACE: BLACKS

	Total Blacks %	Manhattan %	Brooklyn %	21-34 %	35-49 %	50+ %
Prefer black teacher	29	19	38	35	28	17
Prefer white teacher	2	3	1	2	2	3
No difference	66	75	55	60	64	78
Not sure	3	3	6	3	6	2

TABLE 116

TEACHER PREFERENCE BY RELIGION: CITY-WIDE

Religious Affiliation Preferred

	Catholic %	Jewish %	Protestant %	No Difference %	Not Sure %
Total City	11	2	3	79	5
Jewish	--	6	--	90	4
Black	12	2	13	66	7
White Catholic	22	1	--	74	3
Puerto Rican	17	--	--	73	10
White Protestant	4	--	3	90	3

Although 29 percent of blacks said they prefer blacks teaching their children, a much higher 66 percent said it makes no difference. There were some differences within the black community, however, as the breakdown of black opinion on teacher preference by borough and age (Table 115) shows. In Brooklyn, where the dispute centered, 38 percent of the blacks wanted black teachers. Blacks under 35 preferred black teachers rather than whites, amounting to 35 percent. However, a majority among even these groups said that the race of a teacher makes no difference.

While a minority of blacks wanted black teachers in their schools, this demand was not so strong as to seriously threaten to upset the present racial mix among teachers in the city. It does indicate, however, a need to bring more black teachers into the system.

Nor, for that matter, is the question of black teachers a serious problem among whites. Even in the most extreme group surveyed, those who live in areas where the Civilian Review Board was rejected by over 80 percent, only 24 percent expressed a preference that their children be taught by white teachers; none expressed a preference for a black teacher, but 72 percent chose the "no difference" response. Four percent were not sure.

Nor does a preference for teachers of one particular religion run deep in the city, as the data in Table 116 show.

Roughly one in five white Catholics and Puerto Ricans said they prefer Catholic teachers, but among these groups, more than seven in ten said the religion of a teacher makes no difference. Significantly, 66 percent of the blacks said a teacher's religion is immaterial.

Some have argued that a major issue in the Ocean Hill-Brownsville dispute was a deep aversion among blacks to the fact that a majority of the city's teachers are Jewish. All groups were asked to estimate the percentage of Jewish teachers employed in the New York City public schools; the results are shown in Table 117.

All groups were fairly close in their estimate of how many Jewish teachers there are, 61 percent being the median figure.

The same people were asked what percentage of teachers in the city public schools should be Jewish; results are shown in Table 118.

Real differences emerged on this question, the city-wide median coming out at 35 percent, compared with the estimation of 61 percent now in the system. White Catholics, Puerto Ricans, and white Protestants all came out around the city

TABLE 117

ESTIMATE OF HOW MANY JEWISH
TEACHERS ARE IN CITY PUBLIC SCHOOLS

	Median %	Not Sure %
Total City	61	39
Jewish	63	30
Black	62	27
White Catholic	60	44
Puerto Rican	68	58
White Protestant	61	46

average in the number of Jewish teachers they would like to see employed. But blacks only wanted 20 percent, while Jews themselves said 50 percent.

Certainly there is a possibility for some strain between the Jewish and black groups over how many Jewish teachers there should be in New York's schools. That blacks felt only 20 percent of New York City teachers should be Jewish is significant--even the Jewish group wanted to see fewer Jewish teachers in the system. While replacement of any ethnic group in an employment situation with people of other religions or races is a difficult problem, there is something of a mandate for such a policy in these results. The implication is that more black teachers should be phased into the system, especially in black districts. However, wholesale displacement of Jewish teachers would unquestionably exacerbate an already tense situation.

There is another major finding implicit in these results on the educational overtones of the school dispute: The facts indicate that the people of New York City are not nearly as divided in their attitude toward decentralization as might have been expected, considering the amount of heat and racial hatred generated by the dispute itself. On decentralization, a growing trend seems to be developing in support of this principle. However, it is not clear how different groups are defining the term "decentralization." In general, then, if the issue were only decentralization, solution of the school crisis would be within reach. Certainly there is little sign of the same kind of

TABLE 118

ESTIMATE OF HOW MANY JEWISH TEACHERS
THERE SHOULD BE IN CITY PUBLIC SCHOOLS

	Median %	Not Sure %
Total City	35	65
Jewish	50	68
Black	20	40
White Catholic	36	72
Puerto Rican	39	71
White Protestant	35	70

polarization on decentralization as a general principle that was apparent in the racial tensions produced, in part, by the dispute over community control in Ocean Hill-Brownsville.

The question, then, remains: what were the triggers which precipitated the massive outpouring of emotions and even downright hatred in the school controversy? The cross-section of the entire city was asked about key issues in the strike (see Table 119).

On two central issues, a majority of all groups tended to agree: "the teachers' union had to protect the jobs and rights of its members" (agreed to by 56 percent of the blacks) and "blacks wanted to see their kids get a better education" (agreed to by 58 percent of the Jews).

But on four other issues, polarization is immediately apparent. Together they spell out the racial rather than the educational confrontation that the school dispute tragically became.

By an overwhelming 77-9 percent, the Jewish community believed that "blacks in Ocean Hill-Brownsville treated teachers unfairly." Blacks denied this by 51-23 percent. On this charge, a city-wide majority of 51 percent agreed with the Jewish group.

By a lopsided 66-12 percent margin, most Jews felt that "black militant parents and teachers preached anti-Semitism." Blacks disagreed by 40-23 percent, with a relatively high 37 percent not sure. Only 39 percent of the city agreed with the Jewish estimate in this case.

TABLE 119

PERCEPTION OF KEY ISSUES IN TEACHER STRIKE

	Total City %	Jewish %	Black %	Catholic %	Puerto Rican %	White Protestant %
The Teachers Union Had to Protect the Jobs and Rights of Its Members						
Agree	73	88	56	81	54	68
Disagree	9	3	22	3	7	12
Not sure	18	9	22	16	39	20
Blacks Wanted to See Their Kids Get Better Education						
Agree	68	58	90	61	60	75
Disagree	12	24	2	14	6	9
Not sure	20	18	8	25	34	16
Blacks in Ocean Hill-Brownsville Treated Teachers Unfairly						
Agree	51	77	23	61	19	53
Disagree	22	9	51	12	29	13
Not sure	27	14	26	27	52	34
Black Militant Parents/Teachers Preached Anti-Semitism						
Agree	39	66	23	40	13	36
Disagree	22	12	40	20	20	17
Not sure	39	22	37	40	67	47
Teachers Union Spread Stories of Black Anti-Semitism to Get Support in Jewish Community						
Agree	22	19	52	10	12	14
Disagree	34	51	11	46	16	29
Not sure	44	30	37	44	72	57
So Important to Get Community Control, Is Worth Setting Back Child's Education Temporarily						
Agree	18	10	48	11	14	9
Disagree	55	67	30	63	40	65
Not sure	27	23	22	26	46	26

By a heavy 52-11 percent count, most blacks felt that "the teachers' union spread stories of black anti-Semitism to get support in the Jewish community." Jews sharply disagreed by 51-19 percent. But only 22 percent, city-wide, agreed with the blacks on this charge.

By 48-30 percent, blacks said that "it is so important to get community control that it is worth setting back a child's education temporarily." Jews sharply disagreed, by 67-10 percent. So did the city as a whole, by a decisive 55-18 percent margin.

Blacks and Jews both recognized that the other side had legitimate interests at stake. However, each side was strongly divided on the tactics it believed the other to be using. The issues that set loose the flood tide of bitter racial feelings all had to do with the tactics of the dispute rather than the substance of it. None really had much to do with education. The ultimate tragedy is that these tactical differences created so much basic change in New York society.

Significantly, the Jewish reaction to blacks treating teachers "unfairly" was shared by Italians and the Irish in proportions almost as high as among the Jews themselves, as the breakdown in Table 120 shows.

TABLE 120

OPINION: BLACKS IN OCEAN HILL-BROWNSVILLE
TREATED TEACHERS UNFAIRLY

	Agree %	Disagree %	Not Sure %
Total White Catholics	61	12	27
Italian	70	8	22
Irish	74	9	17

The significance of this is that over seven out of ten Jews, Italians, and Irish in New York City have clearly joined common cause in condemning black treatment of the teachers.

On one subject there was real agreement between Jews and Blacks, more than among other groups in the city: that relations

THE NEW YORK CITY SCHOOL DISPUTE 153

between blacks and Jews deteriorated appreciably as a result of the teacher strike. Total city-wide opinion on this subject is shown in Table 121.

That eight in ten Jews, and almost seven in ten blacks, can say that relations between two of New York's key minorities have worsened shows there is deep awareness of the divisions which have resulted from the school confrontation. Whether the damage can be repaired, whether the basic principle of accommodation can be reforged, are two of the most serious questions New York City faces today.

"HARLEM ON MY MIND"

In the middle of the school crisis, in the fall of 1968, the Metropolitan Museum of Art organized a photographic exhibit entitled "Harlem on My Mind." The exhibit itself consisted of a series of period-piece photographs which by themselves would probably not have created much stir within the art community, the black community, or very many other communities in New York City.

But the museum at the same time released the exhibit in book form. A young black girl wrote a commentary about Jews in the foreword of this book, and her comments evoked bitter protests from a number of Jewish organizations. The young black girl's remarks, along with the entire exhibit, became something of a cause célèbre.

Jewish and black people in the survey were asked about "Harlem on My Mind." First, they were asked if they had heard about it, then if the Jewish criticisms were justified, and finally if the remarks of the young black girl were typical of young blacks or not (see Table 122).

A majority of both groups had heard about the controversy --64 percent of the Jews and 51 percent of the blacks. The two groups again split sharply over whether or not Jewish criticism of "Harlem on My Mind" was justified. Jews felt it was justified by 60-14 percent, while blacks familiar with the episode were just as adamant, saying the criticism was unjustified by 58-14 percent. Clearly another episode in the confrontation between blacks and Jews had taken place over "Harlem on My Mind."

Jews familiar with the controversy felt by a narrow 37-31 percent that the young black girl's remarks were not typical of the way other young blacks felt about Jews. But blacks familiar with it said, by 40-29 percent, that the young girl's feelings were shared by most other young black people.

TABLE 121

PERCEPTION OF CHANGE IN BLACK-JEWISH RELATIONS AS RESULT OF TEACHER STRIKE

	Much Worse %	Only Little Worse %	No Effect at All %	Not Sure %
Total City	35	29	15	21
Jewish	49	32	9	10
Black	44	24	15	17
White Catholic	26	32	16	26
Puerto Rican	23	22	22	33
White Protestant	29	32	13	26

TABLE 122

RECOGNITION AND OPINION, "HARLEM ON MY MIND": JEWS AND BLACKS

	Jewish %	Black %
Heard or read about it	64	51
Didn't hear or read about it	36	49
Jewish Criticism of "Harlem on My Mind"		
Justified	60	14
Not justified	14	58
Not sure	26	28
Anti-Jewish Remarks of Black Girl		
Typical of young blacks	31	40
Not typical	37	29
Not sure	32	31

TABLE 123

OPINION OF JEWISH CRITICISM OF "HARLEM ON MY MIND": JEWS

	Justified %	Not Justified %	Not Sure %
Total Jewish	60	14	26
Manhattan	55	17	28
Bronx	58	14	28
Queens	53	15	32
Brooklyn	67	13	20
Orthodox	72	6	22
Conservative	71	3	26
Reform	66	11	23
Non-affiliated	31	36	33
21-34	48	21	31
35-49	59	11	30
Over 50	70	10	20
Under $10,000	65	15	20
$10,000-$15,000	52	16	32
Over $15,000	56	14	30
8th grade	88	3	9
High school	64	10	26
College	51	19	30

There were differences in the Jewish community over how justified the criticism of the exhibit by Jews was, as the breakdown by borough, religious affiliation, age, income, and education shows (Table 123).

A majority of every segment of the Jewish community except the nonaffiliated and the young thought the Jews were justified in condemning the printing of the young girl's remarks. Brooklyn Jews, Orthodox Jews, those who are older, those with less income and less education all felt this more than other groups. Even among the young, a plurality (48-21 percent) felt this way. Only the non-affiliated, by a margin of 36-31 percent, believed Jewish criticism was "not justified."

There is little doubt that if the Jewish community of New York wanted to find confirmation for its suspicions of black anti-Semitism, "Harlem on My Mind" provided the perfect vehicle for it. It is significant that, in spite of differences within the Jewish community, those who tended to defend blacks and to empathize with them were put on the defensive. In the end, by lopsided margins, they, too, with the exception of the non-affiliated, had to admit that "Harlem on My Mind" furthered a sense of unease.

Although only about half of the blacks knew about "Harlem on My Mind," a majority of those thought Jewish criticism to be "not justified" and a plurality thought the girl's comments typical of young blacks. Most blacks seemed unaware of the precarious state of black-Jewish relations and the price that "Harlem on My Mind," together with other events, could cost the black community in its relations with the Jewish people of New York.

VANDALISM AGAINST SYNAGOGUES

There have been a number of cases in New York of synagogues being vandalized, sacred Jewish articles being desecrated, and serious damage being caused by fire. The non-Jewish part of the sample as well as the Jews were asked about this vandalism.

Each group was asked who they thought was responsible for the vandalism; the results are shown in Table 124.

TABLE 124

PERCEPTION OF CAUSE OF VANDALISM AGAINST SYNAGOGUES: JEWS AND WHITES

	Jewish	Non-Jewish Whites	Non-Jewish White "Backlash"
	%	%	%
Isolated young troublemakers	50	56	56
Part of rising anti-Semitism	26	8	15
Plot against Jews	12	5	11
Not sure	12	31	18

THE NEW YORK CITY SCHOOL DISPUTE 157

A majority of all three groups surveyed on the subject attributed the outbreaks to "isolated young troublemakers." However, one in four Jews also saw it as "part of rising anti-Semitism in the city," and another 12 percent saw it as a "plot against the Jews." Few of the non-Jewish white community accepted these two latter alternatives. But a quarter of the special "backlash" sample group saw the attacks on the synagogues either as "rising anti-Semitism" or as a "plot against the Jews."

Clearly, nearly four in ten Jews were seriously disturbed by what they felt was the symptomatic nature of the vandalism. There is no doubt that the acts encouraged the feeling, generated by the school dispute and other incidents, that Jews were under attack on a broad front. Again, Brooklyn Jews and older and less affluent Jews felt most strongly this way.

TABLE 125

INFORMATION ON RACE OF PERSONS ARRESTED
FOR VANDALISM AGAINST SYNAGOGUES

	Jewish %	Non-Jewish Whites %	Non-Jewish White "Backlash" %
Mainly blacks	22	17	19
Mainly whites	12	14	8
Not sure	66	69	73

The city arrested a number of young teenagers, most of whom later confessed to the vandalism. The young culprits were white. People familiar with the vandalism in all three white groups were asked if the vandals were mainly blacks or mainly whites; the percentages are as shown in Table 125.

Most Jews, non-Jewish whites, and those in the non-Jewish white "backlash" sample areas simply could not identify the race of the young people arrested for the vandalism. However, the pattern among those who attempted to identify the young people's race is revealing. Non-Jewish whites split down the middle in making an estimate, which would fit a random or "guesswork" pattern. But by roughly a 2-to-1 margin, non-Jewish whites in the areas which were most anti-Civilian Review Board and Jews answered "mainly blacks," even though no blacks were found to be involved at all.

The point, however, is not the degree of misinformation, but the degree to which over one-fifth of the Jews have become defensive and even skittish about blacks.

When the Jewish group was asked to estimate how much it felt non-Jewish whites were concerned over the vandalism against their synagogues, only one in three Jews (34 percent of the sample) felt that the attacks had evoked concern in the rest of the white community. A larger number, 41 percent, felt that "indifference" had been the non-Jewish white response. The remaining one in four (25 percent) were not sure.

Again, the point is that many Jews in New York City by mid-1969 had begun to feel alienated not only from the black community but also from important parts of the white community.

CHAPTER 6 POTENTIAL AREAS OF CONFRONTATION

BUILDING TRADES EMPLOYMENT FOR BLACKS: POTENTIAL CONFRONTATION WITH NON-JEWS?

Earlier, this study pointed out that a majority of blacks felt they are discriminated against in the skilled labor field, but that most whites did not agree. A particularly difficult area, in the view of blacks, is that of the building trades unions. The unions are most certainly not controlled by Jewish leadership.

Blacks felt deeply that they are discriminated against in this sizable and high-paying area of potential employment, as Table 126 shows.

By a nine-to-one margin, blacks felt discriminated against in the building trades. The college-educated blacks and the more affluent blacks felt most strongly about it.

By a lopsided margin of 64 percent, blacks felt that, compared to other discrimination, discrimination in the building trades is "among the worst" they experience; 6 percent described it as "not as bad," 24 percent as "about the same," and 6 percent as "not sure."

By an overwhelming count of 87 percent, blacks felt that unions in the building trades should be made to accept blacks into apprenticeship programs in the building trades (4 percent were opposed, 9 percent were not sure).

All non-Jewish whites were asked to estimate whether discrimination against blacks is or is not practiced in the building trades. The total response by this sample group, and breakdowns by age, religion, and other factors, are shown in Table 127.

Although 40 percent of the non-Jewish white sample simply were not sure whether discrimination against blacks does exist in this field, by a narrow margin those non-Jewish whites with opinions denied there is discrimination. The young and the college educated in the white community tended to part company

TABLE 126

PERCEPTION OF DISCRIMINATION AGAINST BLACKS BY BUILDING TRADES UNIONS: BLACKS

	Discriminate %	Don't Discriminate %	Not Sure %
Total Blacks	71	8	21
8th grade	48	17	35
High school	74	7	19
College	81	5	14
Under $3,000	45	18	37
$3,000-$6,999	71	8	21
$7,000 and over	83	4	13

TABLE 127

PERCEPTION OF BUILDING TRADES DISCRIMINATION AGAINST BLACKS: NON-JEWISH WHITES

	Discriminate %	Don't Discriminate %	Not Sure %
Total Non-Jewish Whites	28	32	40
21-34	33	29	38
35-49	25	32	43
50+	24	37	39
Catholic	24	36	40
Non-Catholic	39	20	41
Italian	20	46	34
Irish	24	38	38
No college	23	35	42
Some college	42	22	36
Belong to union	25	42	33

POTENTIAL AREAS OF CONFRONTATION 161

from the rest, as, indeed, they did on many other attitudes toward the black community. The non-Catholics also tended to feel discrimination exists, while Catholics did not feel this way. Non-Jewish white union members felt most strongly, along with the Italian group, that there is no discrimination, though the Irish also shared this view to a lesser extent.

Table 128 shows the attitudes on this issue of the special "backlash" sample of non-Jewish whites who voted 80 percent or more against the Civilian Review Board, and gives additional insight into how confrontation might take place in the building trades.

TABLE 128

PERCEPTION OF DISCRIMINATION AGAINST BLACKS
BY BUILDING TRADES UNIONS:
NON-JEWISH WHITE "BACKLASH"

	Discriminate %	Don't Discriminate %	Not Sure %
Total Non-Jewish White "Backlash"	17	49	34
Catholic	15	50	35
Non-Catholic	21	42	37
Italian	15	51	34
Irish	27	42	31
21-34	23	46	31
35-49	8	52	40
50+	17	49	34
No college	14	51	35
Some college	29	41	30
Men	21	54	25
Women	12	43	45
Belong to union	17	56	27
Skilled labor	14	55	31
Unskilled labor	8	56	36

It is apparent that a potential explosion could take place in the building trades area. Real polarization could come between that part of the non-Jewish white community in the sample areas and the blacks. Whites in the "backlash" areas which voted 80 percent or more against the Civilian Review Board felt most strongly--by almost three to one--that blacks are not discriminated against. They also hold probably the most extreme views about blacks generally to be found in all of the city. The skilled and unskilled labor members of this group, as well as the union members and the Italians in the group, felt most strongly that there is no discrimination. Overwhelmingly, blacks saw discrimination in the building trades. They were just about as unanimous on this subject as on any in the survey.

If the issue surfaces, it could become the source of another sort of confrontation--this time between non-Jewish whites and blacks. It could cause polarization to extend to an even broader sector of New York City.

When blacks were asked who runs the building trades unions in New York, more singled out Jews than picked Catholics (see Table 129).

Although over one in two could not identify the leadership of the building trades unions with either Catholics or Jews, the remainder, by 27-20 percent, said that the Jews were running these unions.

Again, as in the case of the Jews' perception of who is responsible for synagogue vandalism, blacks were willing, sight unseen, to pick out the Jews as the group keeping the blacks down. Only in the more affluent black sectors of Queens, among the college educated, and in the higher income brackets did the blacks correctly identify the men running the building trades unions as Catholics or as certainly not Jewish. Such was the state of the polarization on both sides in mid-1969 in New York City.

THE WELFARE CRISIS

Certainly the welfare rolls in New York City have been multiplying enormously. A common complaint among New Yorkers has been that their taxes were going altogether too much for welfare. The bulk of people on welfare in New York City are black. Yet when asked to agree or disagree with the statement "government must provide minimum living standards

TABLE 129

PERCEPTION OF WHO RUNS THE BUILDING TRADES UNIONS: BLACKS

	Mostly Catholic %	Mostly Jews %	Not Sure %
Total Blacks	20	27	53
Manhattan	12	30	58
Bronx	25	36	39
Queens	36	17	47
Brooklyn	18	26	56
8th grade	10	36	54
High school	20	26	54
College	30	20	50
Under $3,000	11	39	50
$3,000-$6,999	19	26	55
$7,000 and over	27	23	50
On welfare	16	34	50
Men	23	30	47
Women	15	26	59

for needy people," New Yorkers overwhelmingly endorsed the principle (see Table 130). Every group supported the general thesis underlying welfare for the needy by better than 7 in 10. In principle, at least, a substantial majority of all groups seems to be in favor of welfare.

Yet blacks and Jews also thought the welfare system is not working right; blacks and Jews agreed that the welfare system is working "only fair" to "poor" (see Table 131). Even those on welfare themselves felt this way.

Most critical of the welfare system in the black community were the more affluent blacks, although a negative feeling was pervasive among all sections of the black community.

In the spring of 1969, the New York State Legislature cut the funds available to New York City for welfare purposes. The cuts evoked instantaneous protests from blacks on welfare and their spokesmen.

TABLE 130

GOVERNMENT MUST PROVIDE MINIMUM LIVING STANDARDS FOR NEEDY PEOPLE: CITY-WIDE

	Agree %	Disagree %	Not Sure %
Total City	79	8	13
Jewish	78	10	12
Black	90	5	5
White Catholic	78	9	13
Puerto Rican	68	6	26
White Protestant	73	11	16
Manhattan	76	6	18
Bronx	87	7	6
Queens	72	15	13
Brooklyn	82	7	11
Richmond	98	2	-

TABLE 131

RATING OF CITY WELFARE SYSTEM: BLACKS AND JEWS

	Excellent %	Pretty Good %	Only Fair %	Poor %	Not Sure %
Total Blacks	8	24	28	32	8
Manhattan	5	22	32	34	7
Bronx	12	24	26	32	6
Queens	2	23	28	38	9
Brooklyn	11	27	25	29	8
8th grade	13	31	27	23	6
High school	8	25	28	30	9
College	4	15	26	50	5
On welfare	15	28	26	27	4
Total Jews	1	10	23	53	12

POTENTIAL AREAS OF CONFRONTATION 165

By only a slim 45-35 percent, people in New York City opposed welfare cuts. The divisions as shown in Table 132 are significant.

TABLE 132

OPINION ON CUTS IN WELFARE FUNDS: CITY-WIDE

	Support Cuts %	Oppose Cuts %	Not Sure %
Total City	35	45	20
Jewish	45	35	20
Black	21	68	11
White Catholic	39	37	24
Puerto Rican	18	57	25
White Protestant	42	36	22
Manhattan	26	56	18
Bronx	27	54	19
Queens	49	31	20
Brooklyn	36	41	23
Richmond	68	26	6

Clearly, the marginal difference was supplied entirely by the blacks and Puerto Ricans, who opposed the cuts by better than 3 to 1. Every other major white ethnic group tended to support the cuts: Jews by 45-35 percent, white Catholics by 39-37 percent, and white Protestants by 42-36 percent. These are not wide margins, but they are perhaps enough to form the basis of another white/nonwhite confrontation in the city.

Among blacks, all segments opposed the cuts, but those blacks actually on welfare opposed the cuts most of all, as the breakdown in Table 133 shows.

The percentages for support and opposition of the more affluent blacks show the beginning of some movement toward following their more affluent white neighbors on the welfare issue, even though a majority opposed the cuts.

TABLE 133

OPINION ON CUTS IN WELFARE FUNDS: BLACKS

	Support Cuts %	Oppose Cuts %	Not Sure %
Total Blacks	21	68	11
Manhattan	19	72	9
Bronx	24	68	8
Queens	34	56	10
Brooklyn	17	69	14
8th grade	18	71	11
High school	20	68	12
College	31	60	9
On welfare	17	79	4

Opposition to cuts in welfare from the black community centered on the "cruelty of making the cuts at a time when the cost of living was reaching record heights" and on the feeling that the people on welfare "really need it." Illustrative was the comment from a 30-year-old black from Brooklyn, who is a corrections officer earning $8,000 a year. He said, "It is shameful to cut the people that need the money, especially when money is spent uselessly on missiles and it is considered OK to waste money if it is the military doing it. But where people get food and shelter, why that is OK to cut. Then they wonder why we are bitter." A black salesman in Queens added, "Why take money away from just those who need it the most? How cruel can you get?" A 66-year-old unskilled black laborer in Harlem said, "Some families can hardly live on the amount they got before. It means some people will go hungry with this latest cut." In the Bedford-Stuyvesant section, a 25-year-old black woman who earns $7,200 working in a stock room said, "It's hard to get by with the rising price of food and shelter as it is. These people couldn't get by before they were cut. What are they to do now?"

All of the volunteered comments by blacks about the welfare cuts add up as shown in Table 134.

TABLE 134

FEELINGS BEHIND VIEWS ON CUTS IN WELFARE FUNDS: BLACKS

	Total Blacks %
Why Support Cuts:	<u>21</u>
Some people should be working, not on welfare	9
Some people should be dropped, jobs found for them	2
My taxes going to people who could work	2
Need new system, this one not working	2
Present system has bad effect on recipients	2
Welfare growing too big, too expensive	1
The deserving don't get it, undeserving do	1
Why Oppose Cuts:	<u>68</u>
High cost of living, not enough to get by on now	29
People really need it, deserve it, need more	16
Deserving people will be hurt, children, old	9
Would mainly cut off blacks who need it	4
People need help to become self-supporting	2
Shouldn't cut without constructive alternative	2
<u>Spending on Vietnam, Space, Foreign Aid, Not on Poor</u>	2
<u>Cut Off Undeserving, Help the Deserving</u>	6
<u>Not Sure</u>	5

The pattern of Jewish opinion on welfare cuts (see Table 135) does not run along the same lines as was evident in racial attitudes.

In the breakdown of Jewish opinion by borough, Queens Jews were most in support of the welfare cuts. Conservative Jews were also, as were those with a high school education. On this issue there is little difference between younger Jews and their elders. Manhattan Jews held to the same pattern as displayed in the breakdown by borough for general racial attitudes; they opposed the cuts, as did non-affiliated Jews. The

TABLE 135

OPINION ON CUTS IN WELFARE FUNDS: JEWS

	Support Cuts %	Oppose Cuts %	Not Sure %
Total Jewish	45	35	20
Manhattan	35	45	20
Bronx	43	37	20
Queens	52	32	16
Brooklyn	46	30	24
Orthodox	47	29	24
Conservative	55	27	18
Reform	48	30	22
Non-affiliated	30	54	16
21-34	47	35	18
35-49	45	37	18
Over 50	45	33	22
8th grade	36	34	30
High school	54	29	17
College	41	40	19

college-educated group was evenly divided for and against the cuts.

A minority of the Jewish community was opposed to the welfare cuts. A 70-year-old shopkeeper in the Bronx earning $7,800 a year put it this way, "It's silly to cut welfare payments when the cost of living is going up. This can only lead to trouble, and God knows we have enough dissatisfied people now without adding to the list." A 24-year-old Jewish graduate student in Manhattan said, "I don't like to see people go hungry. We subsidize farmers, businessmen, and rich industries, but we hate the poor and can't find it in our hearts to help them."

But a plurality supported the cuts, mainly claiming that most of the people on welfare "should be working" and that "it is possible to create jobs for them." A Jewish business executive in Brooklyn, earning $27,000 a year, said, "I'm opposed to welfare. I think people should stand on their own two feet.

TABLE 136

FEELINGS BEHIND VIEWS ON CUTS IN WELFARE FUNDS: JEWS

	Total Jewish[a] %
Why Support Cuts	<u>66</u>
Get them off welfare, should be working	20
Create jobs for people on welfare	19
Cuts will be incentive for them to work	6
Welfare growing too expensive	6
Need new welfare system	6
Present system has bad effect on recipients	4
They were getting too much	3
Deserving don't get it, undeserving get it	2
Why Oppose Cuts	<u>46</u>
A lot of people really need welfare	27
Not enough to get by on now	12
Shouldn't just cut without positive alternative	5
Would mainly cut off blacks who need it	2
Not Sure	<u>7</u>

[a] Total adds to more than 100 percent as some respondents gave more than one answer.

There are certainly enough training centers and the Job Corps available for them to learn something for a change and not live off the fat of the land." A 35-year-old sales clerk in Brooklyn earning $9,200 added, "There are too many people living off our tax money that are healthy but too lazy to work." A 21-year-old district sales manager, making $20,000 in his father's business, said, "People on welfare don't deserve it. If a white person can get out and work, a Negro can go out and do the same amount of work if he only had the get-up-and-go and applied himself."

When the Jewish comments on welfare costs are added up, the result is as shown in Table 136.

To most of the Jewish people who were opposed to the welfare cuts, the state legislature's action marked a failure on the part of establishment society to be concerned with the poor.

The black and Jewish groups were asked to identify, from a list, the agencies or groups they saw as causes that might account for why the welfare cuts came about. The blacks were willing to attribute the blame to every agency and group on the list except "people running welfare department in the city." The blacks' responses are tabulated in Table 137.

The top targets of the black community on the welfare issue were "politicians playing politics with welfare," "the state government," and "the white power establishment."

A majority of the Jewish community attributed the cuts to two causes: "the state government" and "the desire on the part of the public to curb welfare spendings." The Jews' responses are shown in Table 138.

Two other groups were also singled out for blame by the Jewish community--"upstate Republicans" and "politicians playing politics with welfare." However, Jews did not feel that "the white power establishment," "people opposed to helping the poor," or "people who are against black people" were responsible. They shared with the blacks the judgment that "people running the welfare department in the city" were not responsible.

Clearly, the Jewish group, most of whom supported the cuts anyway, saw both a mandate from the public to cut welfare costs and "state government" as the main reasons for the cuts. They categorically turned down the idea that the welfare cuts had racial overtones.

The differences between the Jewish and the black community's interpretation of where the responsibility for welfare cuts lay indicates another potential area of confrontation. The differences are marked and rather deep.

All groups in the city were asked about the merit of welfare recipients protesting the cuts. The summary of opinion is shown in Table 139.

As in the total city weight of opinion on supporting or opposing welfare cuts (Table 132), the city-wide balance on the merit of welfare recipients protesting the cuts emerged as 45-35 percent favorable (see Table 139). However, once again it was the black and Puerto Rican minorities who carried the day against the plurality opposition of Jews, white Catholics, and white Protestants. The breakdown by borough produced a standoff between Manhattan and the Bronx, on one side of the issue, and the other three boroughs.

TABLE 137

VIEW OF CAUSE OF WELFARE CUTS: BLACKS

	Brought About %	Did Not Bring About %	Not Sure %
Politicians playing politics with welfare	69	11	20
The state government	67	8	25
White power establishment	64	16	20
Desire of public to curb welfare spending	63	18	19
Upstate Republicans	62	12	26
People opposed to helping poor	58	23	19
People against black people	56	25	19
People running welfare department in the city	30	47	23

TABLE 138

VIEW OF CAUSE OF WELFARE CUTS: JEWS

	Brought About %	Did Not Bring About %	Not Sure %
The state government	58	9	33
Desire of public to curb welfare spending	57	21	22
Politicians playing politics with welfare	49	20	31
Upstate Republicans	43	18	39
White power establishment	22	48	30
People opposed to helping poor	22	49	29
People against black people	15	57	28
People running welfare department in city	10	60	30

TABLE 139

VIEW OF MERIT OF WELFARE RECIPIENTS PROTESTING CUTS: CITY-WIDE

	More Right %	More Wrong %	Not Sure %
Total City	45	35	20
Jewish	35	46	19
Black	71	18	11
White Catholic	32	44	24
Puerto Rican	56	17	27
White Protestant	35	45	20
Manhattan	59	19	22
Bronx	54	28	18
Queens	32	46	22
Brooklyn	36	44	20
Richmond	30	70	-

TABLE 140

VIEW OF WELFARE RECIPIENTS' TAKING DESPERATE ACTION IF WELFARE UNION STRIKES: BLACKS AND JEWS

	Blacks on Welfare %	Total Blacks %	Jewish %
Justified	50	39	12
Not justified	37	44	73
Not sure	13	17	15

POTENTIAL AREAS OF CONFRONTATION

The survey tested still another possible area of tension over welfare: What might happen if the welfare union called a strike? The possibility is not remote. In fact, it happened twice in the 1960's.

It is possible that once again negotiations might break down, and a walkout take place. If welfare services were either sharply curtailed or stopped, what would be the public's reaction?

The black and Jewish groups were asked if welfare recipients might not be justified to look to desperate, perhaps even violent, action in the event of a strike (see Table 140).

A heavy majority of the Jewish community (73 to 12 percent) and a plurality of blacks (44 to 39 percent) said that they are not sympathetic to welfare recipients' taking drastic action. But among those actually on welfare, approval of desperate action was supported by 50 to 37 percent. (Among young blacks, under 35, approval of militant counteraction was supported 46 to 34 percent.)

Despite the fact that prevailing black opinion would not be in favor of militant countersteps by welfare recipients, the people most likely to be involved, the recipients themselves, would be responsive to appeals to take direct action. Combined with the reaction of the young blacks, certainly it is not overstatement to say that the ingredients are present for a potential confrontation.

The people working in the welfare field are by no means as much drawn from the Jewish community as is the case among schoolteachers. Both the black and Jewish samples were asked for their estimates of whether most of the people running the welfare department, the people working in the department, and the welfare union leaders are Jewish or not; the responses are as shown in Table 141.

A majority of Jews simply were not aware of what Jewish representation is in the welfare field. But in each case, among those with opinions, by roughly a 3-to-1 margin, they did not see their co-religionists making up most of the key people in the welfare field. Between a third and 40 percent of the black group also were not certain about whether most people administering welfare are Jewish. But among those with opinions, by better than 2 to 1, blacks were convinced that the people running the welfare department are Jewish, by a lesser degree (3 to 2) that most people working in the department are Jewish, and by over 3 to 1 that most of the union leaders are Jewish.

Once again, in the welfare field, the differences in perception between the two groups were sharp. Blacks, especially

TABLE 141

ESTIMATE OF HOW MANY JEWS ARE IN WELFARE
DEPARTMENT: BLACKS AND JEWS

	Black %	Jewish %
People Running Welfare Department		
Most are Jews	46	13
Most not Jews	20	31
Not sure	34	56
People Working in Welfare Department		
Most are Jews	38	11
Most not Jews	28	36
Not sure	34	53
Welfare Union Leaders		
Most are Jews	46	9
Most not Jews	14	27
Not sure	40	64

those on welfare, showed themselves deeply upset at the recent cuts. If the situation grows worse, a counterthrust of major confrontation proportions is not inconceivable. A substantial number of blacks were inclined to see the power structure in the welfare field as Jewish rather than black. Thus, still another Jewish-black confrontation could take place in this field, though because of the nature of the union it would probably not begin as a client-professional conflict in the way that the school crisis started as a conflict between parents and teachers.

Part of the problem in the welfare field is that nearly everyone feels that the needy must be taken care of, but virtually no one is willing to give welfare a very high priority. For example, when asked about using tax money for education or for welfare, education was the decisive choice of all groups in the city, including the blacks themselves (see Table 142).

In addition, among substantial numbers of people in the city, there was a feeling that welfare recipients "don't really appreciate the help they receive" (see Table 143).

TABLE 142

OPINION: EDUCATION SHOULD BE GIVEN PRIORITY
OVER WELFARE ON WHERE TAX MONEY GOES

	Agree %	Disagree %	Not Sure %
Total City	65	17	18
Jewish	67	12	21
Black	70	18	12
White Catholic	64	23	13
Puerto Rican	50	20	30
White Protestant	74	13	13
Manhattan	64	16	20
Bronx	58	29	13
Queens	73	12	15
Brooklyn	62	17	11
Richmond	86	14	--

TABLE 143

OPINION: WELFARE RECIPIENTS DON'T REALLY
APPRECIATE THE HELP THEY RECEIVE

	Agree %	Disagree %	Not Sure %
Total City	36	41	23
Jewish	43	35	22
Black	31	52	17
White Catholic	41	34	25
Puerto Rican	21	52	27
White Protestant	39	35	26
Manhattan	27	47	26
Bronx	26	59	15
Queens	46	29	25
Brooklyn	40	37	23
Richmond	62	29	9

TABLE 144

OPINION: PEOPLE RUNNING WELFARE PROGRAMS DON'T REALLY CARE ABOUT PEOPLE ON WELFARE

	Agree %	Disagree %	Not Sure %
Total City	32	43	25
Jewish	20	55	25
Black	56	25	19
Black welfare recipients	64	21	15
White Catholic	27	45	28
Puerto Rican	38	35	27
White Protestant	23	50	27
Manhattan	30	44	26
Bronx	34	48	18
Queens	34	40	26
Brooklyn	31	43	26
Richmond	38	48	14

City-wide, the public disagreed with this proposition by 41 to 36 percent. However, once more it was the combined attitudes of the blacks and Puerto Ricans who made up the critical difference. The Jewish group believed welfare recipients are generally unappreciative by 43 to 35 percent, white Catholics by 41 to 34 percent, and white Protestants by 39 to 35 percent. Again, Manhattan and the Bronx were pitted against the rest of the city, although Brooklyn supported the charge by only a narrow 40 to 37 percent.

The welfare issue sharply splits the city into white and nonwhite. A confrontation in the area would be largely ethnic, and certainly predominantly racial at the outset, but because of Jewish concern over welfare and because of the belief held by many blacks that Jews run the welfare program it could become another black-Jewish division.

For their part, the blacks have developed certain strong conceptions about the people running the welfare programs which separate them from the other groups in the city.

A majority of blacks, 56 to 25 percent, tended to believe that those vested with the responsibility of running the welfare program "really don't care" about the recipients (see Table 144). Significantly, black welfare recipients themselves felt most strongly this way, by 64 to 21 percent. On the other hand, Puerto Ricans agreed by only a slim 38 to 35 percent.

The rest of the city, however, simply tended not to believe the proposition. The group which tended to be most in support of those running the welfare program were the Jews, who denied the proposition by 55 to 20 percent. But substantial pluralities among white Catholics and white Protestants also agreed with the Jewish community that the proposition is not true.

A similar division in city opinion is evident on another proposition: "practically everyone on welfare really needs help and there are only a few chiselers" (see Table 145).

Again, by a narrow margin of 43 to 35 percent city-wide, people agreed with the proposition. But the key difference can be found among blacks, who supported the statement by a sizable 62 to 25 percent. Significantly, white Catholics and white Protestants also endorsed the belief that most people who are on welfare are in real need and that the number who are using it unfairly is small. (The borough-by-borough breakdown is also shown in Table 145.)

Of the ethnic groups in the city sample, the group that was most convinced that there is much chiseling on welfare could be found in the Jewish community, which denied the statement that most people on welfare really need help by 43 to 34 percent. When the answers to the question by Jews are broken down by borough, religious affiliation, age, income, and education, revealing patterns emerge, as shown in Table 146.

The division over welfare is not the same as it was over race, although there are some similarities. By boroughs, Bronx Jews tended to be most sympathetic with welfare recipients. Queens Jews tended to be on the negative side, and Brooklyn Jews again felt most hostile.

Conservative and Reform Jews tended to believe most that welfare recipients are "not really in need of help," more than Orthodox Jews. A plurality of the non-affiliated feel there are only a "few welfare chiselers." The younger age group was most suspicious; however, the college educated felt least strongly the need to deny the claim that welfare recipients, by and large, are in genuine need of help.

The only group as a whole which tended to be more against the welfare program in the city and more suspicious of people on welfare than Jews were those surveyed in the special oversample areas, which voted 80 percent or more against the Civilian Review Board (see Table 147).

TABLE 145

OPINION: PRACTICALLY EVERYONE ON WELFARE
REALLY NEEDS HELP AND THERE ARE ONLY A
FEW CHISELERS

	Agree %	Disagree %	Not Sure %
Total City	43	35	22
Jewish	34	43	23
Black	62	25	13
White Catholic	39	38	23
Puerto Rican	37	25	38
White Protestant	42	40	18
Manhattan	45	26	29
Bronx	55	29	16
Queens	39	43	18
Brooklyn	36	41	23
Richmond	52	36	12

The welfare area is one marked by real cleavages in attitudes. The line-up clearly pits the blacks and the Puerto Ricans on the side of the welfare recipients against sizable pluralities in each of the different sections of the white community. The blacks tended to identify the power structure in welfare with the Jews. Jews, for their part, tended to be more concerned about welfare than were other whites and less sympathetic toward the plight of recipients than were other whites.

Clearly, there is a substantial gap in understanding between the black and the Jewish communities over welfare. The confrontation, however, has not yet taken place there as it has in education. For the sake of black-Jewish relations in the city, such a confrontation must be avoided.

A confrontation over welfare would almost certainly so divide blacks and Jews that, long after the specific issues which triggered the confrontation had been forgotten, the bitterness would linger on.

TABLE 146

JEWISH OPINION: PRACTICALLY EVERYONE ON WELFARE REALLY NEEDS HELP AND THERE ARE ONLY A FEW CHISELERS

	Agree %	Disagree %	Not Sure %
Total Jewish	<u>34</u>	<u>43</u>	<u>23</u>
Manhattan	36	34	30
Bronx	42	36	22
Queens	37	45	18
Brooklyn	26	50	24
Orthodox	25	42	33
Conservative	30	49	21
Reform	33	48	19
Non-affiliated	48	33	19
21-34	29	47	24
35-49	36	43	21
Over 50	36	40	24
Under $10,000	29	43	28
$10,000 - $15,000	43	39	18
$15,000	32	46	22
8th grade	26	44	30
High school	33	46	21
College	37	40	23

NEWS COVERAGE

Many times in the course of the interviews conducted for this study, when asked why they feel changes have taken place, members of all groups volunteered the statement that "the newspapers (or television news) says it's so." Variations on this comment included: "The news media have made a bigger thing out of this than it actually is" and "The news people are always stirring up trouble on these things."

TABLE 147

OPINION ON WELFARE:
NON-JEWISH WHITE "BACKLASH"

	Agree %	Disagree %	Not Sure %
Education should be given priority over welfare on where tax money goes	74	8	18
Welfare recipients don't really appreciate the help they receive	56	25	19
People running welfare programs don't really care about people on welfare	33	41	26
Practically everyone who is on welfare really needs help and there are only a few chiselers	32	54	14

Any assessment of black-Jewish relations in New York City must examine how key groups view the news media. A feeling that newspaper or television news is against you can contribute to a sense of alienation. Needless to say, a sense that they are for you can be reassuring. To feel they are fair and objective can in turn provide a sense of at least some stability in an otherwise highly opinionated and even polarized situation.

All groups in the sample cross-section of adult New Yorkers were asked if they think the newspapers, television, and radio are biased toward the blacks, biased toward the Jews, or are generally fair. The responses are summarized in Table 148.

On a city-wide basis, the central finding is that roughly half the public felt that the news media are fair. The range among the media is 49 percent for television, 51 percent for newspapers, and 52 percent for radio.

Among the one in four people who felt there is bias (roughly one in four could not make a judgment on the media), consistently more New Yorkers felt that the news media are more biased toward the Jews than toward the blacks. The ratios

TABLE 148

PERCEPTION OF NEWS MEDIA BIAS: CITY-WIDE

	Total City %	Jewish %	Black %	White Catholic %	Puerto Rican %	White Protestant %	Non-Jewish White "Backlash" %
Newspapers							
Biased pro-black	9	18	3	11	2	5	21
Biased pro-Jews	17	8	38	7	19	12	5
Fair	51	51	38	54	55	58	51
Not sure	23	23	21	28	24	25	23
Television							
Biased pro-black	11	20	4	12	2	10	21
Biased pro-Jews	15	5	33	6	18	8	4
Fair	49	54	42	56	52	56	53
Not sure	25	21	21	26	28	26	22
Radio							
Biased pro-black	6	12	4	6	--	3	14
Biased pro-Jews	14	4	30	6	13	8	3
Fair	52	55	43	54	54	63	51
Not sure	28	29	23	34	33	26	32

TABLE 149

PERCEPTION OF NEWS MEDIA BIAS: JEWS

	Newspapers				Television				Radio			
	Pro-Black %	Pro-Jewish %	Fair %	Not Sure %	Pro-Black %	Pro-Jewish %	Fair %	Not Sure %	Pro-Black %	Pro-Jewish %	Fair %	Not Sure %
Total Jewish	18	8	51	23	20	5	54	21	12	4	55	29
Manhattan	18	21	31	30	17	15	38	30	13	9	39	39
Bronx	14	9	59	18	16	3	60	21	12	3	58	27
Queens	10	5	64	21	13	5	67	15	5	4	65	26
Brooklyn	26	4	47	23	29	2	49	20	15	2	53	30
Orthodox	26	2	54	18	27	3	53	17	18	2	56	24
Conservative	21	3	53	23	23	-	58	19	13	1	59	27
Reform	20	4	58	18	24	3	56	17	15	2	59	24
Non-affiliated	5	23	39	33	6	14	49	31	2	11	46	41
21-34	12	13	49	26	16	7	53	24	10	6	51	33
35-49	26	13	41	20	26	11	46	17	14	8	50	28
50 and over	18	2	58	22	20	1	59	20	12	-	60	28
8th grade	22	1	52	25	28	-	49	23	18	1	51	30
High school	21	4	55	20	22	5	57	16	11	4	58	27
College	14	14	48	24	16	8	52	24	10	5	53	32

POTENTIAL AREAS OF CONFRONTATION

are 17-9 percent for newspapers, 15-11 percent for television, and 14-6 percent for radio.

However, all of these over-all results hardly begin to tell the real story. Each ethnic group had a vastly different assessment.

Blacks tended to believe that all three media favor the Jewish side. Among those blacks who felt newspapers have a bias, 38-3 percent said it is pro-Jewish; in the case of television, 33-4 percent said it is pro-Jewish; and in the case of radio, 30-4 percent said it is pro-Jewish.

The only other group which consistently agreed with the blacks was the Puerto Ricans, although fewer of them tended to feel there is bias one way or the other.

The Jewish group went in just the opposite direction, tending to feel, where there is bias, it is toward the blacks. They felt most strongly about television (20-5 percent); next most strongly about newspapers (18-8 percent); and least strongly about radio (12-4 percent).

The belief that television is too pro-black was shared to a lesser extent by white Catholics and white Protestants. But the WASP group also leaned slightly the other way on newspapers and radio, believing them to be more pro-Jewish.

The only other group which felt the media are more biased toward the blacks than the Jews were people who lived in the special "backlash" sample areas which voted overwhelmingly against the Civilian Review Board.

Within the Jewish group, there were sharp variations in assessing the news media; as the breakdown by borough, age, and other factors in Table 149 shows.

Brooklyn, Orthodox, middle-aged, and the least well educated Jews felt most strongly that the press, television, and radio are pro-black. By contrast, for example, Manhattan Jews tended to feel that the newspapers are pro-Jewish, television slightly pro-black, and radio slightly pro-black. Young people held the same opinion on newspapers. Non-affiliated Jews who saw bias believed it to be pro-Jewish for all three media.

In all of the foregoing analysis, tendencies have been drawn from a minority of all groups. The fact is that most media in New York City were accepted as being fair. However, tendencies were there. It is safe to conclude that the media were viewed by both the blacks and the Jews as helping their adversaries rather than supporting their own cause. To this extent, the media have encouraged polarization. Easily the most disenchanted with the media were the blacks. But as attitudes harden at the extremes, among the Jews and among the special "backlash" sample group, there may well be a tendency to see even more hostility from the news media. This situation will pose special problems for, and impose special responsibilities on, the news media.

CHAPTER 7 INTERGROUP CONTACT: REAL OR PERCEIVED?

One common explanation of black-Jewish tensions in New York City is that blacks live in ghettos--virtually isolated from the rest of the city except for contact with Jews who hold the strategic positions of control over blacks' lives. The classic example cited is the school system, with a large number of black students and predominantly Jewish teachers. Also, the claim is often made that blacks live in slums operated and owned by Jews.

The study probed in some depth to determine the perceived points of contact between the white community and blacks, and especially between blacks and the Jewish community.

The results obtained by asking each of the groups about its contact with the other show little agreement and wide disparities which can only be attributed to large-scale perception gaps (see Tables 150 and 151).

Close to one in two of the blacks reported that their employer or supervisor at work is Jewish. But only one in six of the Jews said they are an employer or supervisor of blacks.

Nearly four in ten blacks said they have regular contact with Jewish owners or managers of retail stores but no more than one in eight of the Jews said they serve in these capacities in stores where most of the customers are black.

Better than one in four of the blacks said their landlord is Jewish, but less than a fifth of that number (5 percent) of the Jews said they are landlords of buildings occupied by blacks.

In all of these cases, of course, the disparities may not be so much a matter of perception as of reality. For, by definition, one employer or supervisor might be the boss for a larger number of blacks. Similarly, only relatively few Jewish storeowners might be servicing a large number of blacks. And only a handful of landlords might own and operate many buildings occupied by blacks.

TABLE 150

BLACKS' PERCEIVED CONTACT WITH JEWS

Role of Jews with Whom Blacks Report Contact	Have Contact Blacks %	No Contact %	Not Sure %
Employer or supervisor at work	47	49	4
Co-worker at work	43	53	4
Owner or manager of retail store	39	52	9
Teacher or principal in school	31	65	4
Landlord or rent collector	28	65	7
Friend socially	20	77	3
Fellow union member	15	80	5
Neighbor	12	85	3
Employee under black supervisor	2		

TABLE 151

WHITES' PERCEIVED CONTACT WITH BLACKS

Role in Which Whites Report Contact with Blacks	Jews %	Contact Perceived By Non-Jewish Whites %	Non-Jewish White "Backlash" %
Employer or supervisor of blacks at work	16	20	22
Co-worker with blacks at work	54	60	65
Owner or manager of retail store serving blacks	13	6	7
Teacher of blacks in school	18	10	12
Landlord of property blacks live in	5	4	2
Friend of blacks socially	27	38	23
Union member with blacks	24	23	39
Neighbor of blacks	32	42	18
Employee under black supervisor	5	7	6

Although 31 percent of the blacks said they have real contact with Jewish teachers, only 18 percent of the Jewish group said they have contact with blacks through some teaching capacity. Again, it is possible for relatively few Jewish teachers to have contact with large numbers of black children and their parents.

The concept of a small number of one group in a position of authority creating a much larger feeling of contact among those under that authority in other groups is borne out in the case of blacks supervising or employing whites. Although 2 percent of the blacks said they supervise the work of whites, a higher 5 percent of the Jews, 7 percent of the non-Jewish whites, and 6 percent of the special "backlash" sample of whites all said they work under a black supervisor or employer.

But there are areas in which the relationship has to be on a one-to-one basis, and it is in these areas of contact that the real disparities are apparent.

No more than one in eight of the blacks (12 percent) reported that they have contact with Jews as neighbors, but a much higher one in three of the Jews (32 percent) said they have black neighbors. An even higher number of non-Jewish whites (42 percent) reported blacks as their neighbors, although in the special "backlash" sample areas this declined to 18 percent.

While 15 percent of the blacks reported they have contact with Jews as fellow union members, a higher 24 percent of the Jewish group said the same about blacks in their union membership. A high 39 percent in the special "backlash" sample group said they have contact with blacks in their unions.

This disparity narrows a bit in the case of contact in the role of "friends socially." In this case, 20 percent of the blacks said they have contact with Jews, although a higher 27 percent of the Jews said the same about their social contact with blacks. Thirty-eight percent of non-Jewish whites said they are "friends socially" with blacks.

Finally, the largest amount of reported contact among all white groups with blacks was as co-workers at work: 54 percent of the Jews, 60 percent of the non-Jewish whites, and 65 percent of the special "backlash" sample. However, a somewhat lower 43 percent of blacks reported that they have contact with Jews as co-workers.

What at first appears to be rather widespread exaggeration by blacks of contact with Jews as people in authority over much of their lives might well be the reality of the situation. Only a minority of the Jewish community might in fact be in such positions of authority. Yet close to half the blacks might well have contact with these Jews.

TABLE 152

PERCEIVED PERSONAL CONTACT
WITH BLACKS: JEWS

	A Lot %	Some Not a Lot %	Almost None %	Not Sure %
As co-worker at work	22	32	42	4
As neighbor of blacks	10	22	66	2
As supervisor of blacks at work	10	12	73	5
As employer of black domestic	10	18	67	5
As teacher to blacks	9	9	77	5
As employer of blacks at work	8	8	79	5
As union member with blacks	8	16	71	5
As worker in business with black customers	7	12	76	5
As social friend of blacks	6	21	70	3
As owner of business selling to blacks	5	8	84	3
As government employee serving blacks	5	5	86	4
As owner of property blacks live in	2	3	92	3
As employee under black supervisor	2	3	90	5

If this is correct, it obviously places a special burden on these Jews. For it means that much of the black community is apt to judge all Jews by experience with only a minority of the Jewish community. It increases the possibility of blacks obtaining a rather skewed view of Jews from contact with only a minority of that group.

By the same token, the results also point up one of the great ironies of black-white relations in America and of black-Jewish relations in New York City: Clearly, it takes many fewer blacks to convince whites that they have close contact with blacks than it takes whites to convince blacks they are having contact with whites.

The key, of course, is that the common experience in New York of seeing blacks in the course of one's daily life at work or in a neighborhood or in a union or at a social gathering leads whites to report real contact with blacks in these areas.

TABLE 153

PERCEIVED PERSONAL CONTACT WITH BLACKS:
TOTAL NON-JEWISH WHITES

	A Lot %	Some, Not a Lot %	Almost None %	Not Sure %
As co-worker at work	26	34	36	4
As neighbor of blacks	14	28	55	3
As social friend of blacks	11	27	56	6
As supervisor of blacks at work	10	10	72	8
As union member with blacks	10	13	70	7
As worker in business with black customers	7	11	77	5
As employer of blacks at work	6	7	78	9
As teacher to blacks	4	6	83	7
As employer of black domestic worker	4	5	84	7
As owner of business selling to blacks	3	3	87	7
As government employee serving blacks	3	4	88	5
As owner of property blacks live in	2	2	90	6
As employee under black supervisor	2	5	87	6

189

This, in turn, means that most whites, Jewish or non-Jewish, are likely to make generalizations about blacks from those they have some contact with, who are at best only a fraction of the blacks.

Thus, the ultimate irony is that each group, the blacks and the Jews, in New York City have been passing judgments on the other group without either extensive or real contact on a one-to-one, personal basis.

Except in the case of co-employees at work, massive contact between blacks and Jews in New York City really cannot be said to exist. It is, therefore, fair to say that much of the basis for judgments about the other groups is founded on hearsay and on those contact experiences which do not genuinely represent real person-to-person dialogue.

A finer breakdown of the contact pattern with blacks among Jews reveals that what contact there has been has tended to be in the "some but not a lot" category, rather than in extensive contact (see Table 152).

But then the Jewish community's experience has not been very different from that of the non-Jewish white groups; see Table 153 for the report of non-Jewish white perceived contact.

The areas in which Jews registered more extensive contacts with blacks than did the rest of the white community are as teachers (9 percent for the Jews, versus 4 percent for the rest of the whites), as employers of black domestic workers (10 percent, compared with 4 percent perceived by other whites), and as owners of businesses selling to blacks (5 percent, compared with 3 percent, perceived contact by other whites). But for their part, non-Jewish whites reported more extensive social friendship (11 percent, compared with 6 percent for the Jewish group), more extensive perceived contact as neighbors of blacks (14 percent, compared with 10 percent for the Jews), and more extensive perceived contact as co-workers at work (26 percent, versus 22 percent for Jews). The special "backlash" sample group exceeded the other two white samples in reporting extensive contact with blacks in only three categories: having blacks as co-workers (29 percent), being fellow union members with blacks (14 percent), and being employees under black supervisors (3 percent). Table 154 summarizes the perceived personal contact of the "backlash" sample with blacks.

The non-Jewish whites also reported fairly extensive contact with Jews; Table 155 shows the percentages of contact, broken down by religion, ethnic group, education, and union membership. The Italians and the college educated, among

TABLE 154

PERCEIVED PERSONAL CONTACT WITH BLACKS:
"BACKLASH" NON-JEWISH WHITES

	A Lot %	Some, Not a Lot %	Almost None %	Not Sure %
As co-worker at work	29	37	32	2
As union member with blacks	14	25	54	7
As supervisor of blacks at work	7	15	71	7
As teacher to blacks	5	7	83	5
As neighbor of blacks	5	13	78	4
As worker in business with black customers	5	11	78	6
As social friend of blacks	4	19	74	3
As employer of blacks at work	4	7	81	8
As government employee serving blacks	4	4	86	6
As owner of business selling to blacks	3	4	88	5
As employee under black supervisor	3	3	87	7
As employer of black domestic worker	2	5	87	6
As owner of property blacks live in	1	1	92	6

TABLE 155

PERCEIVED PERSONAL CONTACT WITH JEWS:
NON-JEWISH WHITES

	A Lot %	Some, Not a Lot %	Hardly Any %	Not Sure %
Total Non-Jewish Whites	34	35	27	4
Catholic	30	36	29	5
Non-Catholic	45	34	21	-
Italian	44	36	20	-
Irish	30	46	22	2
No college	26	35	34	5
Some college	58	36	6	-
Belong to union	33	33	30	4

the non-Jewish white group, reported substantial contact with Jews. The pattern of degree of contact with Jews among the special sample of "backlash" non-Jewish whites was not substantially different from that reported by the regular non-Jewish white sample (see Table 156). Both groups of non-Jewish whites overwhelmingly felt they have enjoyed "pleasant and easy relations" with Jews (see Table 157).

When asked to describe their relations with Jews, the non-Jewish whites were highly complimentary, as the tabulation of the volunteered responses indicates (Table 158).

The portrait painted by the non-Jewish whites is one which would befit accommodation under the best of circumstances. Of course, it should be pointed out that some of the earlier reported stereotype views of Jews held by the special "backlash" sample group were not entirely conducive to the same easy relationship. It is interesting to note that by a small margin the special sample group of whites who voted 80 percent or more against the Civilian Review Board in 1966 were even more euphoric over their reported relations with Jews than the rest of the white community.

The full roster of black contact with Jews revealed three categories which did not apply in Table 150, in which perceived

TABLE 156

PERCEIVED PERSONAL CONTACT WITH JEWS: "BACKLASH" NON-JEWISH WHITES

	A Lot %	Some, Not a Lot %	Hardly Any %	Not Sure %
Total "Backlash"	35	39	24	2
Catholic	35	40	24	1
Non-Catholic	38	35	26	1
Italian	44	31	24	1
Irish	31	40	29	-
21 - 34	34	46	19	1
35 - 49	35	40	23	2
50 and over	37	30	31	2
No college	32	41	27	-
Some college	51	32	15	2
Men	44	37	17	2
Women	26	41	32	1
Belong to union	41	38	19	2
Skilled labor	32	39	26	3
Unskilled labor	24	45	27	4

TABLE 157

PERCEIVED RELATIONS WITH JEWS: NON-JEWISH WHITES

	Total Non-Jewish Whites %	Total "Backlash" %
Pleasant and easy relations	91	94
Troubles in relations with them	5	3
Not sure	4	3

TABLE 158

FEELINGS BEHIND VIEWS ON RELATIONS WITH JEWS

	Total Non-Jewish Whites[a] %	Total "Backlash"[a] %
Why Pleasant and Easy	96	108
Never had trouble with them	37	48
Some of best friends are Jewish	12	8
No trouble with anybody	12	10
Nice, good people	10	6
Worked, lived with them	7	11
Get on with them very well	6	9
Easy to get along with	4	4
Treat and pay others fairly	2	3
Always willing to help	2	3
Peaceful, nonviolent people	2	3
Pay their bills	1	2
Get on with them better than others	1	1
Why Troubles With Them	5	3
Bad employers	5	2
Bad landlords	-	1
Not Sure	4	3

[a] Totals come to more than 100 percent as some respondents volunteered more than one reason.

TABLE 159

BLACKS' PERCEIVED CONTACT WITH JEWS: ADDITIONAL

	Have Contact %	No Contact %	Not Sure %
Man who collects on credit	14	78	8
Officer of a union	13	81	6
Welfare worker servicing me	7	89	4

TABLE 160

BLACKS' PERCEIVED CONTACT WITH JEWISH EMPLOYER, PRINCIPAL OR TEACHER OR NEIGHBOR

	Jewish Employer %	Jewish Principal or Teacher %	Jewish Neighbor %
Total Blacks	47	31	12
Manhattan	51	28	7
Bronx	42	33	20
Queens	51	47	28
Brooklyn	44	27	8
21 - 34	43	33	13
35 - 49	51	36	13
50+	46	18	9
8th grade	34	18	8
High school	48	31	12
College	56	49	21
Under $3,000	21	23	6
$3,000 - $6,000	51	27	9
$7,000+	57	43	22
On welfare	25	29	8
Men	50	26	12
Women	44	36	13

intergroup contact of blacks with Jews was summarized. The three additional categories are black contact with Jews who collect credit, with Jews as officers of a union, or with Jews as welfare workers servicing them. These three kinds of contact are reported as perceived in Table 159.

Within the black community, a breakdown by borough, age, education, income, and other factors revealed sharp differences on reported contact with Jews in three key categories-- as employers, as principals or teachers, and as neighbors.

In the three key categories of contact, Brooklyn blacks consistently reported the least contact (although Jews in this borough expressed the most apprehension over race), the least well education reported far less contact than the high school or the college educated, the lower income group reported less than the more affluent and those on welfare reported the least contact of all (see Table 160).

The pattern of perceived contact within the black community with Jews parallels the extent to which blacks are affluent. This would indicate that the more educated and more articulate blacks are likely to be more visible to the Jewish community. Those segments which expressed a great likelihood of reacting with violence and more extreme protest in racial confrontations--especially those in the lower income and less affluent parts of black society in New York--have less contact with Jews. It is fair to assume that reactions to Jews from the lower end of the black community is more apt to be based on stereotypes than rooted in actual experience. And where it is based on experience, it is far more likely to be based on contact with Jews who are in a position of authority over blacks.

Blacks were asked to assess the nature of their relations with Jews; the summary of blacks' perception of relations is contained in Table 161.

In most areas, the relationship was reported by blacks to be "easy." The least degree of trouble was reported by blacks when they could count on Jews as "friends socially," as "neighbors," as "fellow members of a union," as "co-workers," as "officers of the union," and, significantly, "when Jews work for me."

Where Jews are reported to be "an employer or supervisor at work," a solid majority of 57 percent of the blacks reported no problems, but one in five (21 percent) did report "trouble." This pattern is paralleled in the case of having contact with Jews as the "owner or manager of a retail store," with 58 percent saying it is an "easy relationship," compared with almost one in four (24 percent) who reported "trouble." By approximately the same percentage, blacks, interestingly, reported "easy relationships" in the "teacher or principal in school" area, despite the friction over Ocean Hill-Brownsville.

But several areas clearly emerge as trouble spots.

Only 37 percent of the blacks were able to say that the relations they have with Jews who are "welfare workers servicing me" are "easy." Twenty-six percent of those reporting this relationship said they have "trouble."

TABLE 161

BLACKS' PERCEPTION OF NATURE OF RELATIONS WITH JEWS[a]

	Easy Relations %	Some Troubles %	Neither[b] %	Both[b] %	Not Sure %
A friend socially	83	5	9	1	2
A neighbor	75	9	14	1	1
Fellow member of a union	71	8	15	1	5
A co-worker at work	65	13	16	2	4
Officer of a union	63	13	12	3	9
Working for me	60	13	20	6	1
Owner or manager of a retail store	58	24	15	1	2
An employer or supervisor at work	57	21	17	2	3
Teacher or principal in school	52	26	14	4	4
Landlord or rent collector where I live	40	39	14	2	5
Welfare worker servicing me	37	26	21	5	11
Man who collects on credit	36	43	17	2	2
Median	60	17	15	2	1

[a] Base: Blacks having contact with Jews in specific capacity.
[b] Volunteered response.

Although 40 percent of the blacks reported an "easy relationship" with their Jewish landlords or rent collectors, just about an equal number, 39 percent, said they have "troubles" in this kind of contact.

Scarcely more than one in three blacks said they get along with the Jewish man who collects on credit, but a larger 43 percent of those reporting this contact said they have "trouble."

It is perhaps no happenstance that the difficult areas in perceived black-Jewish contact all involve either collection of money by Jews from, or Jews giving money to, blacks. Having a Jewish employer might also involve money matters, but there is also an equation of work rendered involved. The three major stress areas were concerned with "getting" or "giving" in the money area. Undoubtedly, such experiences feed the black belief in the stereotype of Jews as being more interested in money than in people.

A closer look at four of the areas in which blacks report "trouble" in contacts with Jews shows that some real differences in perception and experience exist within the black community (see Table 162).

Of the blacks reporting contact with and trouble with a Jewish employer (21 percent), blacks in the Bronx and Brooklyn, those who are younger, those in lower income ranges, and those on welfare reported the highest percentage. The pattern is very different in the relationships with Jews as teachers and principals (26 percent): Queens blacks, younger blacks, the college educated, the middle income group, and those on welfare reported the highest percentage. In the case of a Jewish landlord or rent collector (39 percent), the highest percentages are found among blacks in Queens, those under 35, those with a high school education, those in the middle income bracket, those on welfare, and among black women (who pay bills more often than not). Troubles in relations with Jews as neighbors (9 percent) emerged strongest in Brooklyn and Queens, among the under-35 group, the lower educated and the lower income groups, black men, and among those on welfare (the highest percentage recorded for this relationship).

The blacks who perceive the problem as most severe appear to be centered among welfare recipients on the low end of the scale. Underlying these results is a sense of unease, of having a mixed experience, albeit largely one which they report as tolerable. Ironically, black expectation, as seen earlier, is to be discriminated against, therefore indicating that anything less could be a positive experience. The "trouble," as a number pointed out, is that no black can ever be sure when discrimination will rear its head.

TABLE 162

BLACKS' REPORTS OF "SOME TROUBLE" IN RELATIONS WITH JEWS AS EMPLOYERS, TEACHERS OR PRINCIPALS, LANDLORDS OR RENT COLLECTORS, AND NEIGHBORS

	Troubles With:			
	Jewish Employer	Jewish Principal or Teacher	Jewish Landlord or Rent Collector	Jewish Neighbor
	%	%	%	%
Total Blacks Who Have This Contact with Jews	21	26	39	9
Manhattan	18	20	39	4
Bronx	25	24	42	4
Queens	21	39	54	16
Brooklyn	22	24	34	13
21 - 34	23	34	43	13
35 - 49	23	22	42	6
50+	14	16	21	11
8th grade	19	21	37	15
High school	22	26	42	13
College	19	30	29	4
Under $3,000	27	22	32	10
$3,000 - $6,999	22	33	42	9
$7,000+	18	21	38	9
On welfare	26	28	42	20
Men	22	25	34	13
Women	20	27	43	8

Yet when asked whether they would rather have Jews or non-Jewish whites in the specific roles covered by the study, blacks by and large opted for Jews (see Table 163). The dominant fact to emerge from these results is that, in all cases, blacks could see little difference between dealing with Jewish and non-Jewish whites. However, in nine of the specific roles, those blacks seeing a difference said they would prefer Jews to non-Jews. Only in the cases of a teacher or principal (just two percentage points), a landlord or rent collector (only a three percentage point difference), and the "man who collects on credit" (a sizable 25 to 8 percent "Jewish worse") did the thrust of black opinion turn against the Jews.

This result could be a key finding of this study, for it reveals that most blacks in their own minds did not single out the Jews for criticism in the authority area because they are Jews, but rather because they are whites who happen to be in a position of authority. A rather substantial 22 percent of the blacks, for instance, felt that having Jews "working for me" is better than having other whites under supervision.

The clear implication of these results is that much of the Jewish-black problem stems from the coincidence of contact points, in which Jews have been thrust into authority roles. As such, it is far more a matter of a black-white problem than a Jewish problem. Unfortunately, Jews themselves have taken much of the black thrust as being ethnic in character rather than anti-white. In turn, blacks have also come to adopt more anti-Semitic attitudes, undoubtedly a transference of authority frustrations to the group which so dominantly seems to represent authority to them.

There were differences, however, within the black community itself in this seeming bias in favor of Jewish whites, as shown in the breakdown by age and other factors in Table 164.

A preference for non-Jewish whites could be found only among the under-35 black group. Those in the lower income brackets were evenly divided. The number who said the religion of an employer or supervisor makes no difference clearly rises with education.

In the case of relations with Jewish and non-Jewish white co-workers, once again an overwhelming majority of the blacks said there was no difference.

Table 165 shows that among those blacks with a preference, the young blacks were clearly the least prone to pick a Jewish co-worker as preferable, although, interestingly enough, blacks with an eighth-grade education were most apt to do so.

The black community was asked to choose between a black and a Jew as a contact in certain crucial roles (see Table 166).

TABLE 163

BLACKS' COMPARISON OF RELATIONS WITH JEWS AND NON-JEWISH WHITES[a]

	Jewish Better %	Jewish Worse %	No Difference/ Not Sure %
An employer or supervisor at work	15	10	75
A co-worker at work	12	8	80
Owner or manager of a retail store	13	12	75
Teacher or principal in school	11	13	76
Landlord or rent collector where I live	14	17	69
A friend socially	14	3	83
Fellow member of a union	11	4	85
Man who collects on credit	8	25	67
Officer of a union	10	8	82
A neighbor	17	5	78
Welfare worker servicing me	22	16	62
Working for me	22	-	78

[a] Base: Blacks having contact with Jews in specific capacity.

TABLE 164

BLACKS' COMPARISON OF RELATIONS WITH JEWS AND NON-JEWISH WHITES AS AN EMPLOYER OR SUPERVISOR

	Jewish Better %	Jewish Worse %	No Difference/ Not Sure %
Total Blacks Who Have This Contact with Jews	15	10	75
21 - 34	7	12	81
35 - 49	18	10	72
50+	21	7	72
8th grade	27	8	65
High school	14	12	74
College	13	4	83
Under $3,000	20	20	60
$3,000 - $6,999	14	11	75
$7,000+	15	8	77

TABLE 165

BLACKS' COMPARISON OF RELATIONS WITH JEWS
AND NON-JEWISH WHITES AS CO-WORKER

	Jewish Better %	Jewish Worse %	No Difference/ Not Sure %
Total Blacks Who Have This Contact with Jews	12	8	80
21 - 34	10	9	81
35 - 49	14	8	78
50+	16	5	79
8th grade	20	4	76
High school	12	9	79
College	11	5	84

TABLE 166

BLACKS' PREFERENCE FOR CONTACT WITH
BLACK OR JEW IN SPECIFIC CAPACITIES[a]

	Prefer Black %	Prefer Jew %	Don't Care/ Not Sure %
An employer or supervisor at work	23	11	66
A co-worker at work	26	7	67
Owner or manager of a retail store	29	8	63
Teacher or principal in school	34	6	60
Landlord or rent collector	32	8	60
A friend socially	17	9	74
Fellow member of a union	16	7	77
Man who collects on credit	57	4	39
Officer of a union	20	8	72
A neighbor	29	2	69
Welfare worker servicing me	44	12	44
Working for me	11	--	89

[a] Base: Blacks having contact with Jews in specific capacity.

TABLE 167

BLACKS' PREFERENCE FOR BLACK OR JEW
AS EMPLOYER OR SUPERVISOR

	Prefer Black %	Prefer Jew %	Don't Care/ Not Sure %
Total Blacks Who Have This Contact with Jews	23	11	66
21 - 34	28	7	65
35 - 49	24	10	66
50+	17	16	67
8th grade	17	12	71
High school	25	11	64
College	29	4	67

In all but two of the roles, a solid majority of blacks said that it does not make any difference whether the contact is with a black or a Jew. The two exceptions were "the man who collects on credit," where a rather high 57 percent said they would prefer a black man, compared with only 4 percent who said they would like a Jewish person; and "welfare worker servicing me," where a black was preferred by 44 percent and a Jew by 12 percent.

The differences within the black community on preference for a black or a Jewish employer or supervisor are significant (see Table 167).

The highest backing for having a black supervisor or employer could be found among young blacks and among the most affluent, the college educated. This result is a measure of where the thrust for blacks commanding their own destiny lies in New York: among the young and the most educated.

Yet there is an even more important point here. A majority of all groups of blacks said it makes no difference to them if the major points of contact in their work, in what they buy, in where they live, and in how they run their daily lives are blacks or Jews. This could be taken to mean that there is a large degree of willingness to make accommodations on a racial basis. The problem obviously is not in the racial attitudes of the blacks, but rather in their not having found any way to achieve their objectives short of making white society yield. The fact that the whites who stand at many points of entry to the realm of authority in New York happen to be Jews unquestionably has contributed to polarizing Jewish-black relations.

CHAPTER **8** THE ACTION OPTIONS
OPEN TO
BLACKS AND JEWS

This study was undertaken not merely to explore the current state of black-Jewish relations in New York City, but also to seek those avenues and means which might enable responsible members of both communities to re-establish a sense of accommodation so that the city will not blow apart.

A majority of both blacks and Jews felt free to defend the other at their own meetings, although there was a substantial difference in the percentages (see Table 168).

A clear majority of Jews (67 percent) said that they felt "completely free" to support black demands at Jewish meetings without incurring the wrath of other Jews. However, less than a majority of blacks (46 percent) said they were "completely free" to denounce anti-Semitism at a black meeting. Another 24 percent, however, said they were "somewhat free."

TABLE 168

PERCEIVED FREEDOM TO SPEAK UP IN
SUPPORT OF OTHER GROUP AT OWN
MEETING: BLACKS AND JEWS

	Blacks to Denounce Anti-Semitism %	Jews to Defend Black Demands %
Completely free	46	67
Somewhat free	24	16
Not free at all	16	5
Not Sure	14	12

TABLE 169

PERCEIVED FREEDOM TO SPEAK UP
IN SUPPORT OF BLACK DEMANDS AT
JEWISH ORGANIZATION MEETINGS

	Feel Completely Free %	Feel Somewhat Free %	Feel Not Free at All %	Not Sure %
Total Jewish	67	16	5	12
Manhattan	74	21	1	4
Bronx	74	12	6	8
Queens	74	15	6	5
Brooklyn	55	17	7	21
Orthodox	53	25	5	17
Conservative	60	18	7	15
Reform	80	9	3	8
Non-affiliated	75	12	5	8
21 - 34	74	17	3	6
35 - 49	69	17	5	9
50 and over	61	15	7	17
Under $10,000	58	18	7	17
$10,000 - $15,000	75	17	2	6
$15,000 and over	74	14	5	7
8th grade	49	14	9	28
High school	64	17	6	13
College	75	16	3	6

Within the Jewish community, there were some familiar differences by borough, religious affiliation, and other factors (see Table 169).

Those Jews who ran well below the average on complete freedom to support black demands were residents of Brooklyn, Orthodox Jews, older people, those earning less income, and those with the least education.

It is evident that all of these groups, who consistently have been shown to be most anti-black in this study, also felt some

TABLE 170

PERCEIVED FREEDOM TO SPEAK AGAINST ANTI-SEMITISM AT BLACK ORGANIZATION MEETINGS

	Feel Completely Free %	Feel Somewhat Free %	Feel Not Free at All %	Not Sure %
Total Blacks	46	24	16	14
Queens	57	20	11	12
Brooklyn	36	30	20	14
Under $3,000	40	27	23	10
$3,000 - $6,999	45	24	15	16
$7,000 and over	54	23	12	11
21 - 34	44	25	17	14
35 - 49	49	23	15	13
50 and over	45	22	15	18
Men	50	24	13	13
Women	42	23	18	17
8th grade	45	20	16	19
High school	45	25	16	15
College	53	23	15	9

pressure within their own immediate segment of the Jewish community not to speak up for blacks. However, put into perspective, with the exception of the eighth-grade-educated, a majority of all groups said they were completely free to speak up.

Among blacks, there were also some substantial differences revealed in the breakdown by borough, income, age, and other factors. Majorities of the more affluent, the college educated, and Queens blacks said they feel completely free to defend Jews from attack within their own group, but only 36 percent of the blacks who live in Brooklyn felt the same way. Lower income blacks and black women also reported somewhat less freedom to speak out against anti-Semitism.

Easily the most significant area in which blacks felt most pressures working against their speaking out against anti-Semitism is Brooklyn, where Jews also felt less free. Certainly these results would identify Brooklyn as the target borough in which the greatest tensions and polarization are felt by Jews and blacks alike.

BLACK APPROACHES TO ACTION

Although blacks were aware of Jewish-black tensions, throughout the study it has been evident that they have been less aroused about this subject than about their own frustrations with white society. Only a minority, for instance, have discussed the black-Jewish question with anyone, only one in ten has attended any meetings on the subject, and only one in twenty has taken action on the problem or belonged to an organization which is concerned with the issue (see Table 171).

When the black community is looked at more closely on attendance of meetings on black-Jewish tensions, some sharp dividing lines become apparent (see Table 172).

Clearly, the more affluent part of the black community, especially those who are college educated and live in Queens, has been far more involved in meetings where the subject of black-Jewish tensions has been discussed. For the vast majority of blacks, there has been no exposure to the subject at all in terms of formal meetings. In fact, a majority reported they have not discussed the subject with anyone.

It is fair to conclude that little dialogue has begun within the black community of New York City on the subjects of black-Jewish relations and the implications of the polarization which has taken place.

The cross-section of blacks was asked if they felt certain groups and organizations in New York City have been helpful or not in getting black people a better break in the city (see Table 173).

Only three sources emerged as having at least a plurality of black confidence: the Mayor, who is termed "helpful" by an overwhelming 72-16 percent margin; the city government, believed to be "helpful" by a 52-29 percent division; and the welfare department, given a positive vote of confidence by 44-32 percent.

It is significant that no white institution in New York City outside of the city government is able to evoke a sense of

TABLE 171

ACTIVITY ON BLACK-JEWISH TENSION: BLACKS

	Have %	Have Not %	Not Sure %
Discussed it with anyone	45	54	1
Attended meetings on the subject	10	89	1
Taken any action on the problem	5	93	2
Belonged to a concerned organization	6	93	1

TABLE 172

ATTENDED MEETINGS ON BLACK-JEWISH TENSION: BLACKS

	Have %	Have Not %	Not Sure %
Total Blacks	10	89	1
Manhattan	10	89	1
Bronx	9	90	1
Queens	18	81	1
Brooklyn	8	90	2
21 - 34	12	87	1
35 - 49	12	87	1
50+	5	93	2
8th grade	5	94	1
High school	9	90	1
College	23	76	1
Under $3,000	4	93	3
$3,000 - $6,999	9	90	1
$7,000+	18	82	a
On welfare	8	91	1
Men	12	87	1
Women	9	89	2

[a] Less than 0.5 percent response

TABLE 173

PERCEIVED HELPFULNESS IN GETTING BLACK PEOPLE A BETTER BREAK IN CITY: BLACKS

	Helpful %	Not Helpful %	Neither [a] %	Not Sure %
The Mayor	72	16	4	8
The city government	52	29	5	14
The welfare department	44	32	8	16
The police department	32	47	9	12
White liberals	32	38	7	23
Retail stores where I shop	30	46	10	14
Political leaders	28	44	8	20
My own landlord	27	47	10	16
White people generally	24	48	10	18
Labor unions (not bldg. trades)	22	51	6	21
White store owners	20	57	8	15
Building trades unions	15	59	5	21
White conservatives	13	57	8	22
White real estate agents	11	60	8	21

[a] Volunteered response.

TABLE 174

PERCEPTION OF GROUPS AS MORE LIKELY TO HELP BLACK PEOPLE: BLACKS

	Jews %	Non-Jewish Whites %	Not Much Difference %	Not Sure %
Support local control of schools in black areas	16	12	58	14
Favor open housing	18	8	60	14
Want black people as friends	16	7	63	14
Support demands for separate black community	10	13	60	17
Want blacks to get ahead on a job	17	6	63	14
Willing to work for a black person	11	7	62	20

ACTION OPTIONS OPEN TO BLACKS AND JEWS

confidence from the black community. And, clearly, the Mayor is the personification of this feeling of helpfulness.

In succession, the police department, white liberals, the retail stores shopped in, political leaders, and own landlord, were all rejected by relatively moderate margins as being "not helpful" rather than "helpful" to blacks in getting a better break in New York City. White people generally, labor unions other than those in the building trades, white store owners, the building trades unions, white conservatives, and white real estate agents all met with little confidence from the black community.

The blacks were also asked, who would be more likely to help black people among the whites--the Jewish or the non-Jewish group--in certain substantive issues (see Table 174).

A majority of blacks in each case said that they could see little difference between the Jewish and non-Jewish sources of help. But among the minority of blacks who made a distinction, the balance was more favorable toward Jews than non-Jews. Most notably, blacks would expect Jewish help to be more likely in support of open housing, in wanting black people as friends, and in wanting blacks to get ahead on the job. There was one exception: on the issue of supporting demands for a separate black community, blacks tended to feel by a slight margin that non-Jews would be more helpful than Jews.

Again, as in the case of contacts in their daily lives, blacks certainly cannot be cast in the role of being more hostile toward Jews than toward other whites. To the contrary, if there is any direction in their perception of differences in the white community, blacks in the survey showed themselves more apt to look to Jewish rather than non-Jewish support.

Within the black power structure, a great many groups and individuals have made claims to leadership roles in the past few years. The survey asked blacks which ones they respected. The results showed a clear order of confidence within the black community (see Tables 175 and 176).

National organizations, such as the Southern Christian Leadership Conference and the National Association for the Advancement of Colored People (NAACP), headed the list in New York, as, indeed, they have previously among blacks nationally. The Urban League and the Congress of Racial Equality also ranked well up in confidence levels.

Down toward the middle of the list, Haryou Act, the Welfare Rights Committee, and the Harlem Rent Committee all emerged with moderate support. The Revolutionary Action

TABLE 175

RESPECT BLACK LEADERS AND ORGANIZATIONS: BLACKS

	A Great Deal %	Some-what %	Not A Great Deal %	Not Sure %
Southern Christian Leadership Conference	62	24	6	8
NAACP	60	27	9	4
Shirley Chisholm	58	20	7	15
Urban League	49	32	9	10
Rhody McCoy	45	28	11	16
CORE	43	33	10	14
Whitney Young	43	29	11	17
Roy Wilkins	43	25	14	18
James Farmer	38	31	14	17
Adam Clayton Powell	37	32	20	11
Percy Sutton	31	32	13	24
Floyd McKissick	29	32	15	24
Harlem Rent Committee	29	31	14	26
Haryou Act	29	33	18	20
Welfare Rights Committee	28	34	12	26
Kenneth Clark	28	27	10	35
Stokely Carmichael	28	31	25	16
Bayard Rustin	26	31	17	26
Roy Innis	25	29	13	33
Jesse Gray	22	35	18	25
Livingston Wingate	20	28	16	36
Leslie Campbell	20	26	14	40
Rap Brown	19	30	32	19
Ron Karenga	14	23	17	46
Revolutionary Action Movement (RAM)	14	24	33	29
Herb Callendar	12	23	11	54
Julian Mayfield	12	23	12	53
Herman Ferguson	12	24	19	45
Five Percenters	11	21	29	39
Robert "Sonny" Carson	10	22	12	56
Lincoln Lynch	9	24	13	54
Sol Herbert	5	21	12	62

TABLE 176

RESPECT BLACK LEADERS AND ORGANIZATIONS
A GREAT DEAL: BLACKS

	Total Blacks %	Age 21-34 %	Age 35-49 %	Age 50 & Over %	Under $3000 %	$3000-$6999 %	Over $7000 %
Southern Christian Leadership Conference	62	56	65	71	56	60	70
NAACP	60	55	62	69	56	60	63
Shirley Chisholm	58	56	64	55	44	52	72
Urban League	49	43	49	60	43	46	57
Rhody McCoy	45	47	48	35	25	45	56
CORE	43	45	44	40	36	41	51
Whitney Young	43	36	46	48	31	38	59
Roy Wilkins	43	36	49	45	29	42	55
James Farmer	38	32	43	38	25	34	52
Adam Clayton Powell	36	32	39	38	28	36	40
Percy Sutton	31	25	35	36	24	30	38
Floyd McKissick	29	28	32	24	15	26	41
Harlem Rent Committee	29	29	29	26	27	29	29
Haryou Act	29	30	29	27	25	29	30
Welfare Rights Committee	28	28	30	27	32	28	24
Kenneth Clark	28	26	31	26	17	24	42
Stokely Carmichael	28	37	24	19	20	26	35
Bayard Rustin	26	23	30	24	13	24	40
Roy Innis	25	27	25	20	17	22	31
Jesse Gray	22	23	24	16	13	22	26
Livingston Wingate	20	21	24	20	18	21	27
Leslie Campbell	20	21	21	15	15	19	23
Rap Brown	19	27	17	8	16	20	21
Ron Karenga	14	17	14	9	9	14	17
Revolutionary Action Movement (RAM)	14	18	14	10	22	16	9
Herb Callendar	12	12	12	13	9	12	15
Julian Mayfield	12	12	12	11	8	10	15
Herman Ferguson	12	12	13	11	11	12	13
Five Percenters	11	15	9	8	16	12	8
Robert "Sonny" Carson	10	10	11	8	7	10	11
Lincoln Lynch	9	10	8	8	6	10	11
Sol Herbert	5	4	5	6	3	6	5

Movement received only scattered support. The Five Percenters finished even lower down.

Four individual blacks stood out from the rest. Well at the top of the list was Congresswoman Shirley Chisholm, elected in 1968 from Bedford-Stuyvesant. She was followed by Rhody McCoy, who was a major figure in the Ocean Hill-Brownsville struggle, and two moderate black leaders, Whitney Young and Roy Wilkins. In turn, they were followed by James Farmer, Adam Clayton Powell, Percy Sutton, Floyd McKissick, and Kenneth Clark, who received moderate support.

The first of the militants to emerge on the list is Stokely Carmichael, who finished at about the middle of the list. He was followed by Bayard Rustin, Roy Innis, Jesse Gray, Livingston Wingate, Leslie Campbell, Rap Brown, and Ron Karenga. While all of these men have different outlooks and positions, several of them tended to be more militant and to be more associated with black power movements than most of those who ranked higher on the list. Finally, those with least visibility were Herb Callendar, Julian Mayfield, Herman Ferguson, Robert "Sonny" Carson, Lincoln Lynch, and Sol Herbert. This group represents a variety of views, and all seem to have finished down toward the bottom more from a lack of name-visibility than in terms of any rejection of their views.

Three differences within the black community should be noted. First, such well-known militants as Stokely Carmichael, Rap Brown, and Ron Karenga received more respect among the young blacks than among older blacks. For example, 28 percent of all blacks said they respect Carmichael a "great deal"; the proportion rises to 37 percent among those 21-34 years old. Looking at the same point from a different perspective: though they have substantial support among young blacks, most of those moderate leaders and organizations who were reported as respected "a great deal" (the Southern Christian Leadership Conference, the NAACP, the Urban League, Whitney Young, and Roy Wilkins, for instance) were given more support among older blacks. Rhody McCoy is the only leader receiving a "great deal" of respect by more than one-third of the blacks and also receiving his greatest support from the young.

Second, blacks earning less than $3,000 a year tended to have a "great deal" of respect for leaders and organizations less often than those with higher incomes. Only the Welfare Rights Committee, the Revolutionary Action Movement, and the Five Percenters received more respect from low income blacks than those with higher incomes.

ACTION OPTIONS OPEN TO BLACKS AND JEWS 215

Third, without exception, polarization has taken place over the militants, who have a minority of supporters, generally counterbalanced by a substantial body of critics.

Looking at the list of black leaders as a whole, there is little doubt that the mainstream of blacks in New York looks for the type of leadership personified by the late Martin Luther King, Jr. rather than that typified by Stokely Carmichael. This does not mean that blacks are unmilitant in their demands or that they are prepared to let up in the intensity of their objectives. It does mean that the so-called black militants have made less penetration and have a much smaller power base within the New York black community from which to operate, though they have developed a good deal of support among the young.

The blacks surveyed were queried for their opinions on a series of statements about difficulties in New York City (see Table 177).

The results have both positive and negative implications. On the positive side, by 89-5 percent, blacks agreed that "if we are going to survive in this city, Jews and blacks, Catholics and Protestants--all of us--better learn to get along together." They also agreed with the statement that "the real bigots like nothing better than to see Jews and blacks at each other's throats" by 77-7 percent. They agreed that Jewish rabbis and leaders have been right to urge Jews not to be anti-black by 75-10 percent. And they agreed with the efforts of black ministers and less extreme black leaders who have tried to show Jews that blacks are their friends, by 74-6 percent.

By sizable pluralities, blacks also agreed that the city government has gone to great lengths to try to improve black-Jewish relations (45-32 percent agree) and supported, perhaps surprisingly, the proposition that "unless Jewish leaders and groups put the anti-Jewish black militants in their place, there will be a lot more anti-Semitism" (44-33 percent agree). The implication of this last statement is that blacks are by and large not opposed to steps taken against black militants, although it is important to note that less than a majority of blacks were willing to go that far, and that one in three disagreed. However, the question is a good test of how most blacks feel when confronted with efforts to stem anti-Semitism, on the one hand, and protecting black militants on the other.

Black suspicions about Jews in the economic area did emerge in decisive proportions. Sizable majorities of blacks felt that "the power structure among Jews wants to protect its economic interests even if it means keeping others down," agreed to by 73-13 percent.

TABLE 177

OPINION ON DIFFICULTIES IN NEW YORK CITY: BLACKS

	Agree %	Disagree %	Not Sure %
If we are going to survive in this city, Jews and blacks, Catholics and Protestants--all of us--better learn to get along together	89	5	6
The real bigots like nothing better than to see Jews and blacks at each other's throats	77	7	16
Jewish rabbis and leaders have been right to urge Jews not to be anti-black	75	10	15
Black ministers and less extreme leaders have tried to show the Jews that blacks are their friends	74	6	20
The power structure among Jews wants to protect its economic interests even if it means keeping others down	73	13	14
The city government has gone to great lengths to try to improve black-Jewish relations	45	32	23
Unless Jewish leaders and groups put the anti-Jewish black militants in their place, there will be a lot more anti-Semitism	44	33	23

ACTION OPTIONS OPEN TO BLACKS AND JEWS

Blacks were saying in their reactions to these statements that they generally applaud genuine efforts to defuse black-Jewish tensions, even though they held suspicions about the economic motives of Jews in general and the Jewish power structure in particular. Clearly, there was not much concern among most blacks that these suspicions tend to encourage tension rather than relieve it. Blacks might say that, since in their view Jews control many of the power authority points which affect black society until the blacks' economic plight is improved, they will continue to view Jewish motives with some suspicion. If any real change can be demonstrated positively, and if this change can be related to Jewish authority points, the result can only be a lessening of today's tensions.

But blacks were also aware of the other side of the coin: that by attacking each other, both blacks and Jews are likely to be worse off (see Table 178).

When asked why they felt this way, blacks pointed out that "fighting never helps, but makes things worse," and "we need each other and must live and work together." As a keypunch operator in Harlem put it, "If we attack each other, we are regressing. Blacks are trying to progress, not regress. By attacking, we all regress together." A 27-year-old black technician, who earns $6,800 a year in the south Bronx, said, "It will be chaos if we attack one another. The Jews have all the power and the black man will fight for what he believes in. Man, we really need each other." A black office manager in Brooklyn added, "The two of us will kill each other, destroy ourselves, and then there won't be none of any of us left."

When all of the volunteered reasons among blacks are added up, the results are as shown in Table 179.

If blacks are unprepared to give up a number of the shibboleths about Jews which they feel are rooted in reality, at least they showed themselves to be largely aware of the consequences of further Jewish-black polarization.

The blacks were asked what might be the most effective way to ease black-Jewish tensions (see Table 180). Three main suggestions emerged:

1. "Having groups of Jews and blacks get together." Here blacks were saying that a dialogue between the two groups might be most helpful.

2. "Electing better public officials." This reinforces the pattern seen before, that blacks tend to look to the city government, the Mayor, and other key public officials rather than to the private sector for help.

TABLE 178

VIEW OF EFFECT OF BLACKS AND JEWS ATTACKING EACH OTHER: BLACKS

	Total Blacks %
Both worse off	66
Not much difference	22
Not sure	12

TABLE 179

FEELINGS BEHIND VIEW OF BLACK-JEWISH ATTACKS: BLACKS

	Total Blacks %
Both Worse Off	**81**
Fighting never helps, makes things worse	34
We need each other, must work and live together	15
We should try to understand, respect each other, have peace	8
Jews have power, will get back at blacks	7
Others against both blacks and Jews, should save our strength	5
Mostly the blacks will be worse off	5
Increases tension, hatred between us	5
Jews help, give blacks jobs	4
Fighting distracts from more important issues	3
Not Much Difference	**8**
To get somewhere, blacks have to fight anyway	3
Things won't change anyway	3
Blacks must be independent, not depend on Jews	2
Not Sure	**6**

TABLE 180

VIEW OF MOST EFFECTIVE WAY TO IMPROVE
BLACK-JEWISH RELATIONS: BLACKS

	Total Blacks %	Man. %	Brx. %	Quns. %	Bklyn. %	Under $3,000 %	$3,000 to $6,999 %	$7,000 and Over %
Having groups of Jews and blacks get together	54	66	53	53	46	43	57	56
Electing better public officials	49	67	37	34	45	37	52	53
Speak out against all hostile statements from other side	33	45	16	24	33	24	38	30
Demonstrations	26	36	21	17	23	20	31	19
Write letters to responsible officials	25	35	22	17	21	28	24	24
Boycotts	23	31	17	6	23	15	28	19
Strikes	21	28	15	7	23	15	27	15
Sit-ins	18	28	12	7	17	14	23	18
Other	4	6	5	4	3	6	2	4
None	3	5	1	1	3	4	2	2
Not sure	7	7	3	6	9	8	7	4

TABLE 181

CONFIDENCE IN LEADERS RESOLVING BLACK-JEWISH
TENSIONS: BLACKS and JEWS

	Black View			Jewish View		
	Will Do Something %	Won't Do %	Not Sure %	Will Do Something %	Won't Do %	Not Sure %
Black organizations	79	10	11	48	30	22
The Mayor	80	13	7	36	50	14
Ministers	80	12	8	52	27	21
Priests	76	14	10	52	28	20
Rabbis	72	17	11	65	20	15
Jewish social action organizations	62	21	17	67	17	16
City government officials	61	27	12	33	45	22
Black militant leaders	38	45	17	8	75	17
Political party leaders	53	31	16	30	46	24

219

3. "Speak out against all hostile statements from the other side." Here blacks were saying that efforts to increase tension should be undercut as rapidly as possible. And while the denial usually has difficulty catching up with the charge, blacks in effect were saying that it is better to have an answer than to let the charge remain unchallenged.

Minorities of blacks cited "demonstrations," "boycotts," "strikes," and "sit-ins" as ways of improving black-Jewish tensions, but these approaches finished well below the more temperate recommendations.

Both Jews and blacks were asked how much confidence they had in various leadership sources resolving black-Jewish tensions (see Table 181).

It is significant that, from the black side, all but one of the groups on the list received majority support in terms of being likely candidates for relieving black-Jewish tensions. The one exception was "black militant leaders," rejected by the blacks by 45-38 percent.

Compared with the narrow degree of confidence blacks were willing to grant in terms of helping blacks realize their demands, these results indicate that the black community in New York is perhaps far more open to a dialogue and action programs to alleviate black-Jewish tensions than many might have imagined. It is significant, for example, that blacks were more hopeful about the roles of priests, rabbis, city government officials, and political party leaders than were Jews. In general, blacks had more confidence that something would be done by those leaders. The difference between blacks and Jews is especially marked over the role of the Mayor and, to a slightly lesser extent, the city government and politicians in general.

The real question, of course, will be the degree to which black leaders with substantial followings in New York City are willing to undertake concrete and dramatic programs which try to elicit the support of the broader community. Once this accommodation at the top has taken place, then the black community would have to be reached, perhaps in a way which has not been done by mixed black and white groups before.

APPROACHES WITHIN THE JEWISH COMMUNITY

Significantly, within the Jewish community, there was far less optimism on the likelihood of elements in the power structure really having an impact on black-Jewish tensions.

ACTION OPTIONS OPEN TO BLACKS AND JEWS

As Table 181 indicates, most Jews were doubtful of the role which might be played by the Mayor, city government officials, political party leaders, and, most of all, black militants. Jews were also less sanguine than blacks about what ministers, priests, and rabbis could do.

The only area in which Jewish expectations exceeded those of blacks is in the category "Jewish social action organization"; these organizations occupy powerful roles in the New York City community. Jews were most optimistic about these organizations by a 67-17 percent margin. (Blacks also expressed confidence in these Jewish organizations by 62-21 percent.)

The non-Jewish community, by and large, saw some urgency in re-establishing relations between the two groups which have so recently polarized (see Table 182).

TABLE 182

VIEW OF JEWISH-BLACK RELATIONS:
NON-JEWISH WHITES

	Total Non-Jewish Whites %	"Backlash" Sample %
Should be closer together	62	49
Should be further apart	5	10
Don't care [a]	14	23
Not sure	19	18

[a] Volunteered response.

By a decisive 62-5 percent, the white non-Jewish sectors believed there should be a rapprochement. However, when the special "backlash" sample group was asked the same question, only 49 percent said they would like to see the two groups work closer together; 10 percent said the two groups should be further apart; and a rather high 41 percent said "don't care" or "not sure."

Although the non-Jewish white sector of New York tended to feel some urgency about the necessity to repair the rupture and to re-establish a modicum of accommodation, clearly there were elements in that community which were either

TABLE 183

PERCEPTION OF JEWISH RABBI OR ORGANIZATION LEADER URGING JEWS NOT TO BE HOSTILE TO BLACKS: JEWS

	Happened %	Didn't Happen %	Agreed %	Did Not Agree %
Total Jewish	11	89	8	3
Manhattan	8	92	5	3
Bronx	13	87	8	5
Queens	14	86	12	2
Brooklyn	8	92	6	2
Orthodox	13	87	10	3
Conservative	11	89	9	2
Reform	12	88	10	2
Non-affiliated	8	92	3	5
21 - 34	7	93	4	3
35 - 49	13	87	9	4
50 and over	12	88	10	2
Under $10,000	9	91	7	2
$10,000 - $15,000	8	92	6	2
$15,000 and over	11	89	9	2
8th grade	10	90	8	2
High school	11	89	9	2
College	11	89	7	4

oblivious to the situation or not averse to seeing blacks and Jews remaining adversaries.

The Jewish group was asked to report on its perception of some of the developments which have taken place on the issue of black-Jewish relations within the Jewish community. One question concerned the incidence of a rabbi or organizational leader urging Jews not to be hostile to blacks. Those who said they had been witnesses to such events were then asked if they agreed or disagreed with the urging (see Table 183).

TABLE 184

PERCEPTION OF JEWISH RABBI OR ORGANIZATION LEADER TELLING ABOUT ANTI-SEMITIC ACTIVITY AMONG BLACKS: JEWS

	Happened %	Didn't Happen %	Agreed %	Did Not Agree %
Total Jewish	13	87	9	4
Manhattan	12	88	7	5
Bronx	15	85	12	3
Queens	14	86	9	5
Brooklyn	11	89	9	2
Orthodox	15	85	15	-
Conservative	13	87	10	3
Reform	10	90	8	2
Non-affiliated	14	86	3	11
21 - 34	12	88	6	6
35 - 49	17	83	13	4
50 and over	11	89	10	1
Under $10,000	10	90	6	4
$10,000 - $15,000	11	89	6	5
$15,000 and over	17	83	14	3
8th grade	7	93	4	3
High school	9	91	8	1
College	17	83	12	5

Only one in nine Jews reported recalling that a rabbi or organizational leader had urged Jews not to be hostile to blacks. Apparently such an occurrence was more common in the Bronx and Queens, but was not especially frequent since there was no pronounced pattern.

For the most part, when such an urging took place, however, most Jewish listeners were impressed. For every three who did not agree with what the rabbi or leader said, there were eight who did agree.

The Jewish group was asked about an opposite kind of occasion, one in which a rabbi or leader told about anti-Semitic activity on the part of blacks (see Table 184).

Again, the incidence of perception of such an event was relatively low. The affluent tended to recall such an occasion more than the less affluent. Significantly, the ratio of "agreed" responses to "did not agree" responses among people who recalled a rabbi or organization leader telling them of black anti-Jewish activity was almost precisely the same as to a rabbi or leader admonishing a Jewish group not to be hostile to blacks.

While it is true that people tend to rationalize the kind of meetings they choose to attend--in that they tend to go to those where they expect to hear a point of view sympathetic to their preconceived notions--nonetheless the thrust of these results indicates that rabbis and organizational leaders can have an impact on their Jewish constituencies.

When asked what activities they had engaged in which dealt with Jewish-black tensions, a sizable number of Jews reported having been involved (see Table 185).

Over 7 in 10 Jews in the city said they had discussed the polarization, 12 percent said that they had gone to meetings on the subject, 9 percent said they had taken some action on it. The more affluent reported being the most active, along with Jews under 35. Reform Jews and the non-affiliated had been the busiest, while Orthodox Jews had been the most dormant. The less well educated had not been actively involved. Brooklyn Jews had discussed it more but had done less formally about it, and Manhattan Jews had been most oblivious to the problem.

It is apparent that, although a majority of Jews in the city have discussed the problem of black-Jewish tensions, the affluent and the Reform and non-affiliated Jews were the most active. The groups who have been least active on the subject are the same ones who, throughout this study, are shown to be the most prone to anti-black feelings.

The Jewish community was given a list of Jewish leaders and organizations and asked which it respected and in what degree (see Table 186).

A number of organizations emerged as highly respected by most Jews in New York: the Federation of Jewish Philanthropies was at the top, followed by the United Jewish Appeal, Israel Bonds, B'nai B'rith Grand Lodge, ORT (Organization for Rehabilitation through Training), Hadassah, the Anti-Defamation League, and the American Jewish Congress.

TABLE 185

ACTIVITY ON JEWISH-BLACK TENSIONS: JEWS

	Discussed It %	Gone To Meetings %	Taken Action %	Belong To Concerned Organization %
Total Jewish	71	12	9	10
Manhattan	59	5	7	6
Bronx	72	15	8	8
Queens	75	16	11	17
Brooklyn	74	10	8	8
Orthodox	62	6	5	6
Conservative	69	11	5	10
Reform	82	12	9	10
Non-affiliated	71	19	17	14
21 - 34	76	12	12	12
35 - 49	71	16	12	13
Over 50	67	10	4	7
Under $10,000	63	5	3	3
$10,000 - $15,000	76	15	14	15
Over $15,000	75	17	11	16
8th grade	61	4	-	-
High school	71	10	6	7
College	74	16	13	15

These were followed by the New York Board of Rabbis, the Zionist Organization of America, and the American Jewish Committee.

By and large, Jewish organizations outstripped specific individuals in respect as well as recognition. Easily the most respected figure in the Jewish community was former Justice Arthur Goldberg. He was followed by Albert Shanker, the United Federation of Teachers President, then by Mrs. Herbert Lehman, Rabbi Joachim Prinz, and Rabbi Louis Finkelstein.

TABLE 186

RESPECT FOR JEWISH LEADERS AND ORGANIZATIONS: JEWS

	A Great Deal %	Some- what %	Not A Great Deal %	Not Sure %
Federation of Jewish Philanthropies	62	24	5	9
United Jewish Appeal	61	26	6	7
Arthur Goldberg	58	26	6	10
Israel Bonds	52	28	8	12
B'nai B'rith Grand Lodge	49	27	10	14
ORT	49	29	6	16
Hadassah	47	34	8	11
Anti-Defamation League	44	30	12	14
American Jewish Congress	41	30	11	18
New York Board of Rabbis	38	30	12	20
Albert Shanker	34	33	19	14
Zionist Organization of America	34	29	15	22
American Jewish Committee	30	29	11	30
Mrs. Herbert Lehman	28	28	9	35
Rabbi Joachim Prinz	21	19	6	54
Rabbi Louis Finkelstein	17	15	6	62
Dore Schary	16	20	9	55
Judge Bernard Botein	14	16	6	64
Rabbi Menachem Schneyerson	11	11	5	73
Rabbi Israel Miller	11	11	4	74
Shad Polier	10	13	6	71
Lubavich Hasidim	9	10	9	72
Irving Mitchell Felt	7	9	5	79
Mayer Kahane	7	9	4	80
Arnold Foster	6	6	4	84
Lawrence Wien	6	7	3	84
Will Maslow	5	7	3	85
Morris Eisendrath	5	7	4	84
Rabbi Kelman	5	8	3	84
Charles Bassire	4	6	5	85
Ben Buttenweiser	3	6	4	87

ACTION OPTIONS OPEN TO BLACKS AND JEWS

The Jewish community clearly has been accustomed to look to its active organizations for leadership. Certainly the more the leading organizations representing all parts of the Jewish community are welded together to address this common problem of black-Jewish tensions, the more effective will be the effort to alleviate the problem. The study also included black opinions on counterpart groups and organizations in the black community with which Jewish organizations work directly (see Tables 175 and 176). One real advantage of the Jewish social action groups is that they are highly respected by blacks and Jews alike.

The Jewish cross-section was asked to give a reaction to each of a series of statements describing attitudes toward black-Jewish tensions in New York City (see Table 187). As was evident in the responses of blacks to a series of similar statements, there are a number of positive signs in the responses.

By an almost unanimous 93-3 percent, Jews in New York City agreed that "if we are going to survive in New York City, Jews and blacks, Catholics and Protestants, all better learn to get along together." They were even more convinced (85-5 percent) than the blacks that "real bigots like nothing better than to see Jews and blacks at each other's throats." They also endorsed the statement that "Jewish rabbis and leaders have been right to urge Jews not to be anti-black."

By the same token, the Jewish group rejected three propositions which in themselves could exacerbate the situation. For example, by 52-34 percent, they rejected the notion that "with ambition of blacks and competition for good jobs, the rest of us will have to look out for ourselves." By 52-29 percent, they also turned down the statement that "with blacks pushing as they are, it may be a good idea to move into neighborhoods with our own kind of people." And by 53-26 percent, they did not endorse the statement that "rich Jews can afford to defend blacks, but those less well off who are threatened by blacks cannot."

However, on two counts, Jews responded in an essentially negative direction. First, by 65-24 percent, they agreed with the statement that "city government has gone too far in the direction of giving in to black demands." Clearly, most Jews have become suspicious of New York City's government, particularly on this sensitive issue. By a majority of 59-23 percent, most Jews also said they believe that "unless Jewish leaders and groups put anti-Jewish black militants in their place, there will be a lot more anti-Semitism."

TABLE 187

OPINIONS ON TENSIONS IN NEW YORK CITY: JEWS

	Agree %	Disagree %	Not Sure %
If we are going to survive in New York City, Jews and blacks, Catholics and Protestants better learn to get along together	93	3	4
Real bigots like nothing better than to see Jews and blacks at each other's throats	85	5	10
Jewish rabbis and leaders have been right to urge Jews not to be anti-black	78	7	15
City government has gone too far in the direction of giving in to black demands	65	24	11
Unless Jewish leaders and groups put anti-Jewish black militants in their place, there will be a lot more anti-Semitism	59	23	18
With ambition of blacks and competition for good jobs, rest of us will have to look out for ourselves	34	52	14
With blacks pushing as they are, it may be good idea to move into neighborhoods with our own kind of people	29	52	19
Rich Jews can afford to defend blacks, but those less well off who are threatened by blacks cannot.	26	53	21

ACTION OPTIONS OPEN TO BLACKS AND JEWS

A breakdown by age and education on Jews' reactions to black competition reveals where the pressures from the rising black thrust were felt as a threat (see Table 188). Among older Jews and those with the least education, there was some feeling that "with ambition of blacks and competition for good jobs, the rest of us will have to look out for ourselves."

But the responses which point out the real target of Jewish disaffection came on the statement that "unless black militants are put in their place, there will be a lot more anti-Semitism" (for breakdowns by borough, religious affiliation, age, and education on this statement, see Table 189).

In the borough-by-borough breakdown, the highest percentage of agreement occurs among Brooklyn and Bronx Jews. In the breakdown by affiliation, Orthodox Jews agree most strongly that black militants must be put "in their place," followed by Conservative Jews. On an age basis, Jews over 50 years of age were far more apprehensive than were those under 35. Those Jews with the least education feared black militants the most, while the college educated worried about them least. Only the non-affiliated Jews disagreed with the statement, by a plurality of 49 to 33 percent.

It is apparent that Jewish fears over black militants taking a tack of anti-Semitism is close to the center of the trigger that sets off polarization. These Jews want the militants repressed. Blacks are not basically sympathetic with the black militants, but would undoubtedly interpret Jewish efforts against them as anti-black. Clearly, there is leadership which is respected by both the Jews and blacks which does not fit into the black militant category. Indeed, it might be possible to persuade some black militants that it is not to their or to anyone else's advantage to have the Jewish and black communities tearing each other apart. More than anything else, however, it is evident that the Jewish people of New York need to see a type of black leadership emerge which does not echo the strident anti-Jewish sentiments which have been expressed during the past few years. For its part, the Jewish community must find ways of selecting out and differentiating types of black leadership and black thinking. To categorize all black leadership or all blacks as bigoted toward Jews obviously is to invite more polarization and conflict between the two groups.

When Jews were asked what ought to be done to relieve Jewish-black tensions, the rank order of the responses paralleled that among blacks to the same list of possible solutions (see Table 190).

TABLE 188

JEWS' PERCEPTION: WITH BLACK COMPETITION
WE HAVE TO LOOK OUT FOR OURSELVES

	Agree %	Disagree %	Not Sure %
Total Jewish	34	52	14
21 - 34	29	58	13
35 - 49	30	58	12
50 and over	40	43	17
8th grade	41	34	25
High school	41	44	15
College	25	63	12

At the top of the list, mentioned by 49 percent of the Jewish community as most effective, was "having groups of Jews and blacks get together." It is evident that substantial numbers of Jews would also like to see a dialogue commenced and continued, not only on the leadership level, but also among other groups--young people, older people, borough residents, and neighborhoods. Jews also saw importance in "electing better public officials," although in 1969 they might not see eye to eye with the blacks on this score. The third most frequently mentioned approach was "speaking out against all hostile statements from the other side."

Although the frequency with which Jews considered each measure to be most effective is below those for blacks, the rank order of what Jews and blacks want is remarkably parallel. Both, it would appear, are open to the same sorts of approaches, provided the beginning is really made.

A FINAL OBSERVATION

All of the groups in the survey were asked if they agree or disagree that, in order to survive as a city, all groups had better learn to get along with each other (see Table 191).

In the past, accommodation among the city's minority groups has kept the city together. Accommodation has served

TABLE 189

JEWS' PERCEPTIONS: UNLESS BLACK MILITANTS PUT IN THEIR PLACE, WILL BE LOT MORE ANTI-SEMITISM

	Agree %	Disagree %	Not Sure %
Total Jewish	59	23	18
Manhattan	46	34	20
Bronx	65	20	15
Queens	58	26	16
Brooklyn	65	15	20
Orthodox	77	12	11
Conservative	68	14	18
Reform	58	17	25
Non-affiliated	33	49	18
21 - 34	51	32	17
35 - 49	59	27	14
Over 50	67	12	21
8th grade	69	11	20
High school	67	15	18
College	50	33	17

as a kind of glue, but, as this study has shown, in mid-1969 this glue was partially dissolved.

This study has revealed a tendency toward polarization in this city--with the issue of race dividing Manhattan from Brooklyn, dividing younger from older New Yorkers, dividing the affluent from the less affluent, dividing the college educated from the less well educated. It has raised the possibility of two New Yorks, similar to the two Americas--with the young, the affluent, the college educated, and blacks on one side; and with the older, less well educated white New Yorkers on the other side.

One of the most striking findings of this study has been the change in attitudes as a result of black-Jewish conflict and confrontation among a substantial section of the Jewish community, in the past in the forefront of liberalism and tolerance

TABLE 190

VIEWS OF MOST AND NEXT MOST EFFECTIVE WAYS
OF RELIEVING JEWISH-BLACK
TENSIONS: JEWS

	Most Effective %	Next Most Effective %
Having groups of Jews and blacks get together	49	20
Electing better public officials	36	22
Speaking out against all hostile statements from the other side	17	21
Writing letters to responsible officials	11	15
Demonstrations	4	6
Boycotts	3	5
Strikes	2	4
Sit-ins	1	3
None	4	6
Not sure	10	13

in New York. This change makes possible an alliance between this section of the Jewish community and much of the rest of the white community, particularly the large Catholic group. Should other confrontations occur, blacks would be able to muster support from Puerto Ricans and some backing from white Protestants and from the young and the college educated in all groups.

But to contemplate choosing up sides is to expect or to believe that a state of war exists. Such is not yet the case. Suspicion of blacks lies deep in major segments of the Jewish community. But as the answers to the question of who Jews consider more of a threat, blacks or non-Jewish whites (Table 100), make clear, the section of the Jewish community which feels fundamentally threatened by blacks is still a minority. The center of this feeling is in Brooklyn, among Orthodox Jews, among the less privileged, less affluent, and older people. This part of the Jewish community is almost balanced

TABLE 191

CITY-WIDE OPINION: TO SURVIVE IN CITY,
ALL BETTER GET ALONG

	Agree %	Disagree %	Not Sure %
Total City	88	5	7
Jewish	93	3	4
Black	89	5	6
White Catholic	87	5	8
Puerto Rican	70	11	19
White Protestant	91	4	5
Manhattan	84	6	10
Bronx	86	8	6
Queens	89	4	7
Brooklyn	90	4	6
Richmond	98	-	2

off by Manhattan, Queens, non-affiliated, younger, and more affluent Jews. In the middle are Bronx Jews, Reform Jews, and those between 35 and 49. In the survey they showed themselves genuinely worried by the black thrust in the city but not yet ready to abandon their tradition of backing the underdog.

The most hopeful sign in this study is that New York City, always a city of minorities, still looks at itself as such. The answers to the question of surviving in New York make an important point: despite all that has happened in New York City, its major groups overwhelmingly believe that survival requires getting along with each other--in other words, accommodation.

If either the Jewish or the black community is judged by what is most visible or most vocal, then accommodation will not work, and the city will be doomed to become an armed camp, filled with escalating confrontations in a wider and wider substantive area. Welfare might be the next source of confrontation, though it could also come in a number of other areas.

The key element which must be accommodated, of course, is the black thrust for achieving equality--not the promise of it, but now. This does not mean that whites in New York must comply with all black demands, but the gaps in understanding of how it is to live as blacks live in New York must be filled in.

The number of blacks in the population of New York is rising, as is the number of Puerto Ricans. A city which is approaching one-third nonwhite can ill afford to be divided on racial lines. Either it mobilizes its resources to move the entire city forward, or it will become ever more dangerously divided.

These might sound like dire warnings, but the results of this study clearly show that New York's basic problem now lies in the attitudes of each of its minority groups. The emotions of the past few years must be overcome. This most important city in the country must find a way of accommodating its nonwhite citizens as it has accommodated so many other groups in the past.

ABOUT THE AUTHORS

LOUIS HARRIS is President of the public opinion research firm, Louis Harris and Associates. He has been engaged in the field of public opinion research for 24 years, as a partner to Mr. Elmo Roper and since 1956 as president of his own firm. In the past 14 years he has conducted over 1,000 surveys covering a wide spectrum of marketing, industrial, financial, and governmental research as well as a number of major social and psychological studies.

Mr. Harris writes a political and public opinion column that is published twice a week in 140 newspapers across the U.S. He is the author of the book *Is There a Republican Majority?* and co-authored *The Negro Revolution in America* and *Black and White.*

Mr. Harris is a graduate of the University of North Carolina where, since 1964, he has had a non-salaried appointment on the Political Science Faculty and where the Louis Harris Data Center has been set up by the University.

BERT E. SWANSON is Professor of Political Sociology, Sarah Lawrence College, and Co-Director of the Consortium on Community Crisis, Cornell University-Sarah Lawrence College. He has assisted public officials at the federal, state, and local levels in the areas of health, education, housing, and race relations.

Mr. Swanson is the author of *The Concern for Community in Urban America* and *The Struggle for Equality: School Integration Controversies in New York City.* He is a co-author of *The Rulers and the Ruled: Political Power and Impotence in American Communities* and edited *Current Trends in Comparative Community Studies.* Mr. Swanson has also written numerous articles in the fields of education and sociology.

Dr. Swanson received his B.A. from George Washington University and his M.A. and Ph.D. from the University of Oregon.